nickelodeon

降击神通

AVATAR

THE LAST AIRBENDER

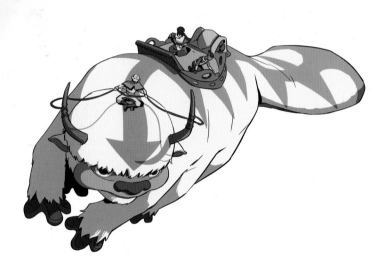

nickelodeon™

降击神通

AVATAR

THE LAST AIRBENDER™

KATARA AND THE PIRATE'S SILVER

Script
FAITH ERIN HICKS

Art
PETER WARTMAN

Colors
ADELE MATERA

Lettering
**RICHARD STARKINGS &
COMICRAFT'S JIMMY BETANCOURT**

DARK HORSE BOOKS

president and publisher
MIKE RICHARDSON

editor
RACHEL ROBERTS

assistant editor
JENNY BLENK

collection designer
SARAH TERRY

digital art technician
SAMANTHA HUMMER

martial arts consultant and model
TODD BALTHAZOR

Special thanks to Linda Lee, James Salerno, and Joan Hilty
at Nickelodeon, to Dave Marshall at Dark Horse, and to Bryan
Konietzko, Michael Dante DiMartino, and Tim Hedrick.

Published by **Dark Horse Books**
A division of **Dark Horse Comics LLC**
10956 SE Main Street | Milwaukie, OR 97222

DarkHorse.com
Nick.com

To find a comics shop in your area,
visit ComicShopLocator.com

First edition: October 2020
eBOOK ISBN 978-1-50671-714-2 | ISBN 978-1-50671-711-1

1 3 5 7 9 10 8 6 4 2
Printed in China

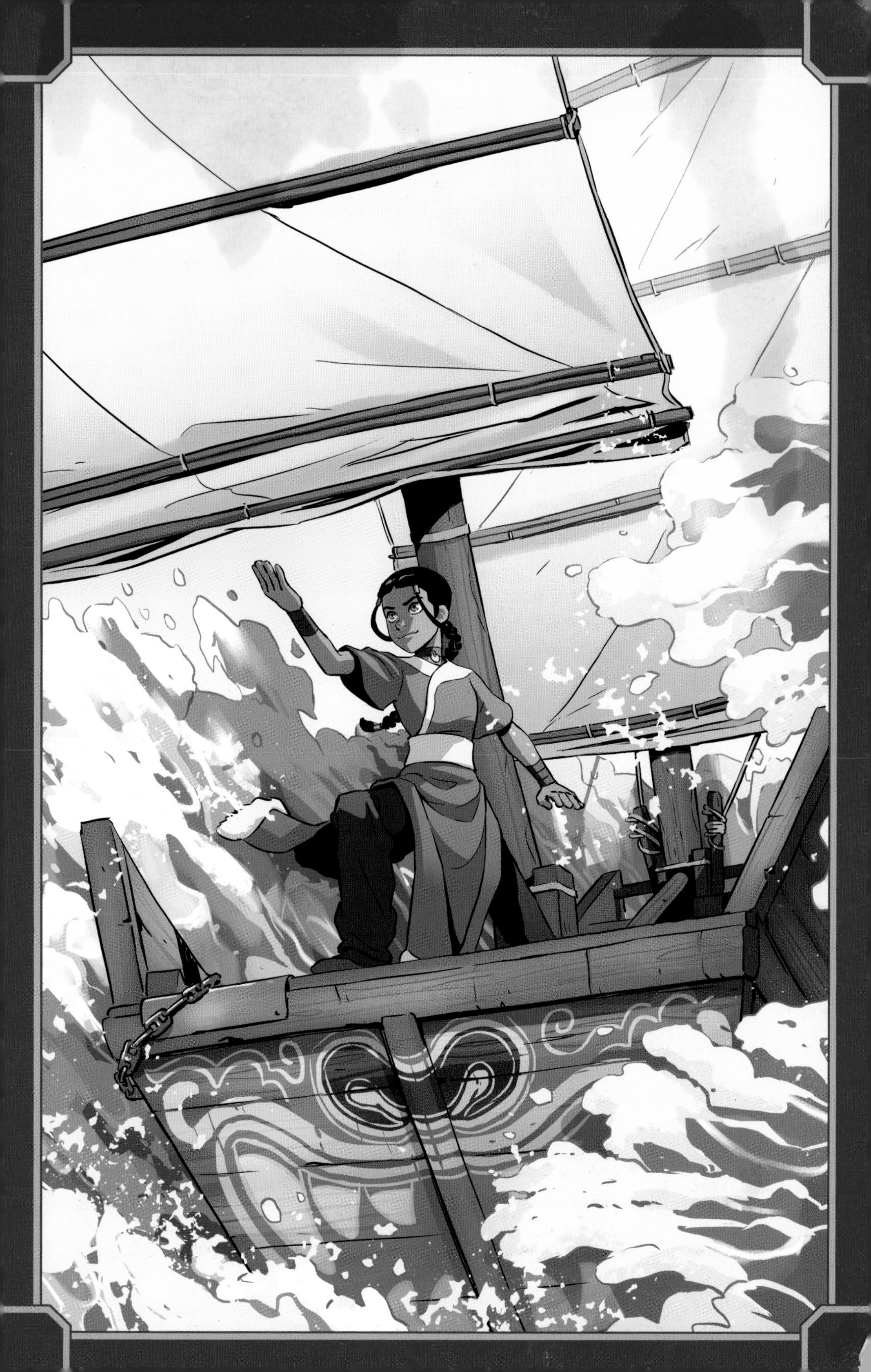

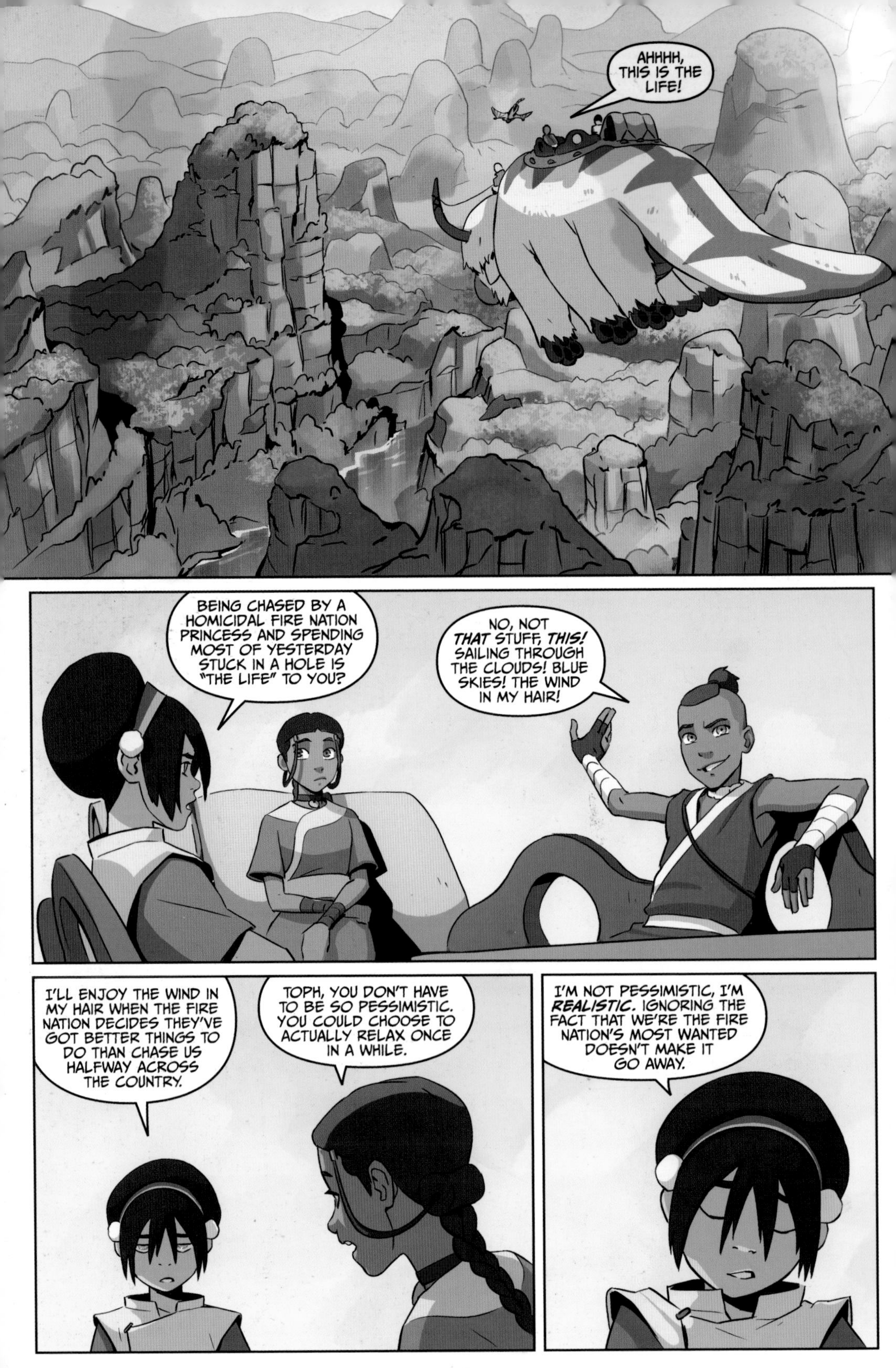
AHHHH, THIS IS THE LIFE!
BEING CHASED BY A HOMICIDAL FIRE NATION PRINCESS AND SPENDING MOST OF YESTERDAY STUCK IN A HOLE IS "THE LIFE" TO YOU?
NO, NOT *THAT* STUFF, *THIS!* SAILING THROUGH THE CLOUDS! BLUE SKIES! THE WIND IN MY HAIR!
I'LL ENJOY THE WIND IN MY HAIR WHEN THE FIRE NATION DECIDES THEY'VE GOT BETTER THINGS TO DO THAN CHASE US HALFWAY ACROSS THE COUNTRY.
TOPH, YOU DON'T HAVE TO BE SO PESSIMISTIC. YOU COULD CHOOSE TO ACTUALLY RELAX ONCE IN A WHILE.
I'M NOT PESSIMISTIC, I'M ***REALISTIC.*** IGNORING THE FACT THAT WE'RE THE FIRE NATION'S MOST WANTED DOESN'T MAKE IT GO AWAY.

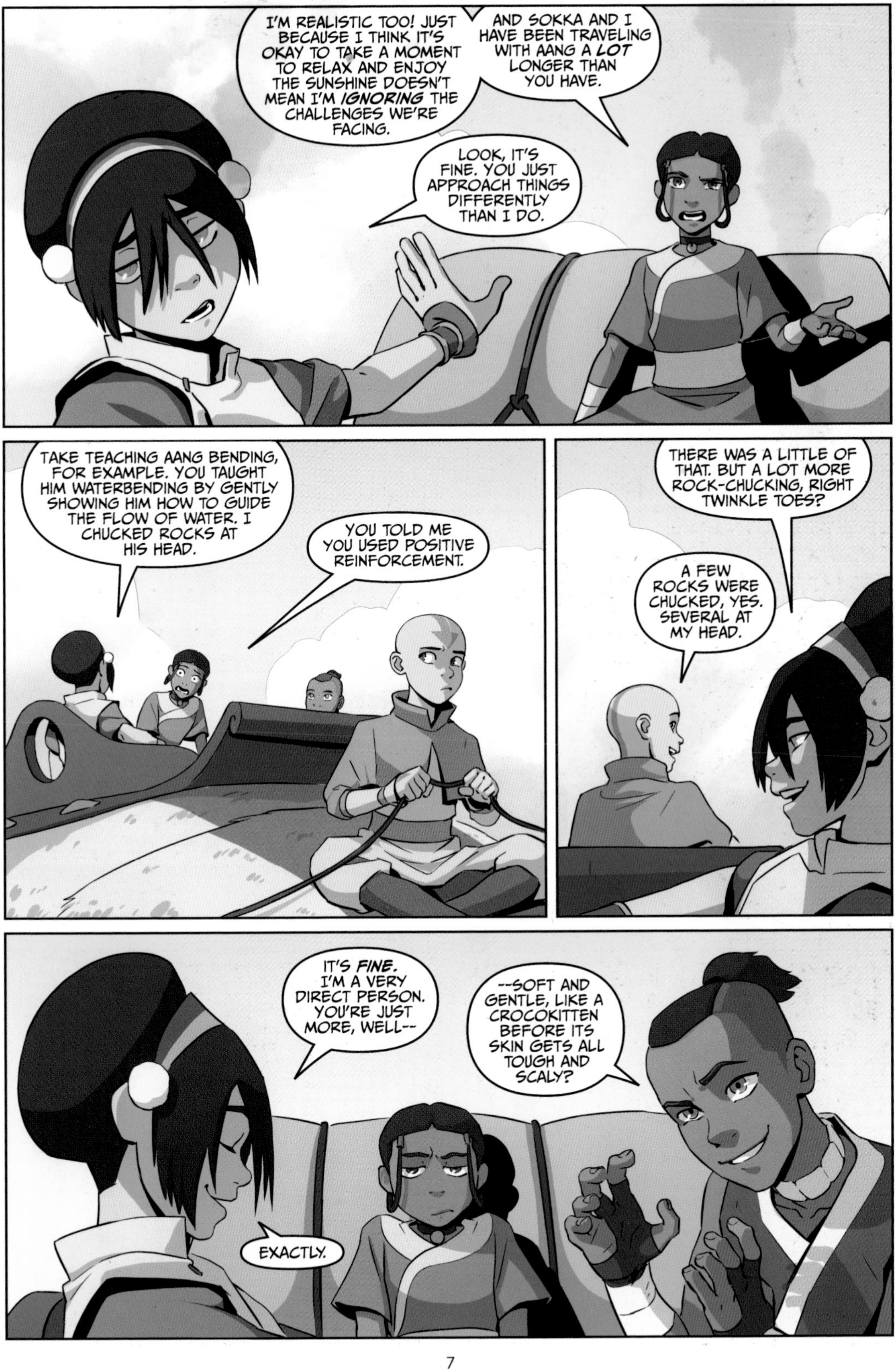
I'M REALISTIC TOO! JUST BECAUSE I THINK IT'S OKAY TO TAKE A MOMENT TO RELAX AND ENJOY THE SUNSHINE DOESN'T MEAN I'M *IGNORING* THE CHALLENGES WE'RE FACING.
AND SOKKA AND I HAVE BEEN TRAVELING WITH AANG A *LOT* LONGER THAN YOU HAVE.
LOOK, IT'S FINE. YOU JUST APPROACH THINGS DIFFERENTLY THAN I DO.
TAKE TEACHING AANG BENDING, FOR EXAMPLE. YOU TAUGHT HIM WATERBENDING BY GENTLY SHOWING HIM HOW TO GUIDE THE FLOW OF WATER. I CHUCKED ROCKS AT HIS HEAD.
YOU TOLD ME YOU USED POSITIVE REINFORCEMENT.
THERE WAS A LITTLE OF THAT. BUT A LOT MORE ROCK-CHUCKING, RIGHT TWINKLE TOES?
A FEW ROCKS WERE CHUCKED, YES. SEVERAL AT MY HEAD.
IT'S *FINE.* I'M A VERY DIRECT PERSON. YOU'RE JUST MORE, WELL--
--SOFT AND GENTLE, LIKE A CROCOKITTEN BEFORE ITS SKIN GETS ALL TOUGH AND SCALY?
EXACTLY.

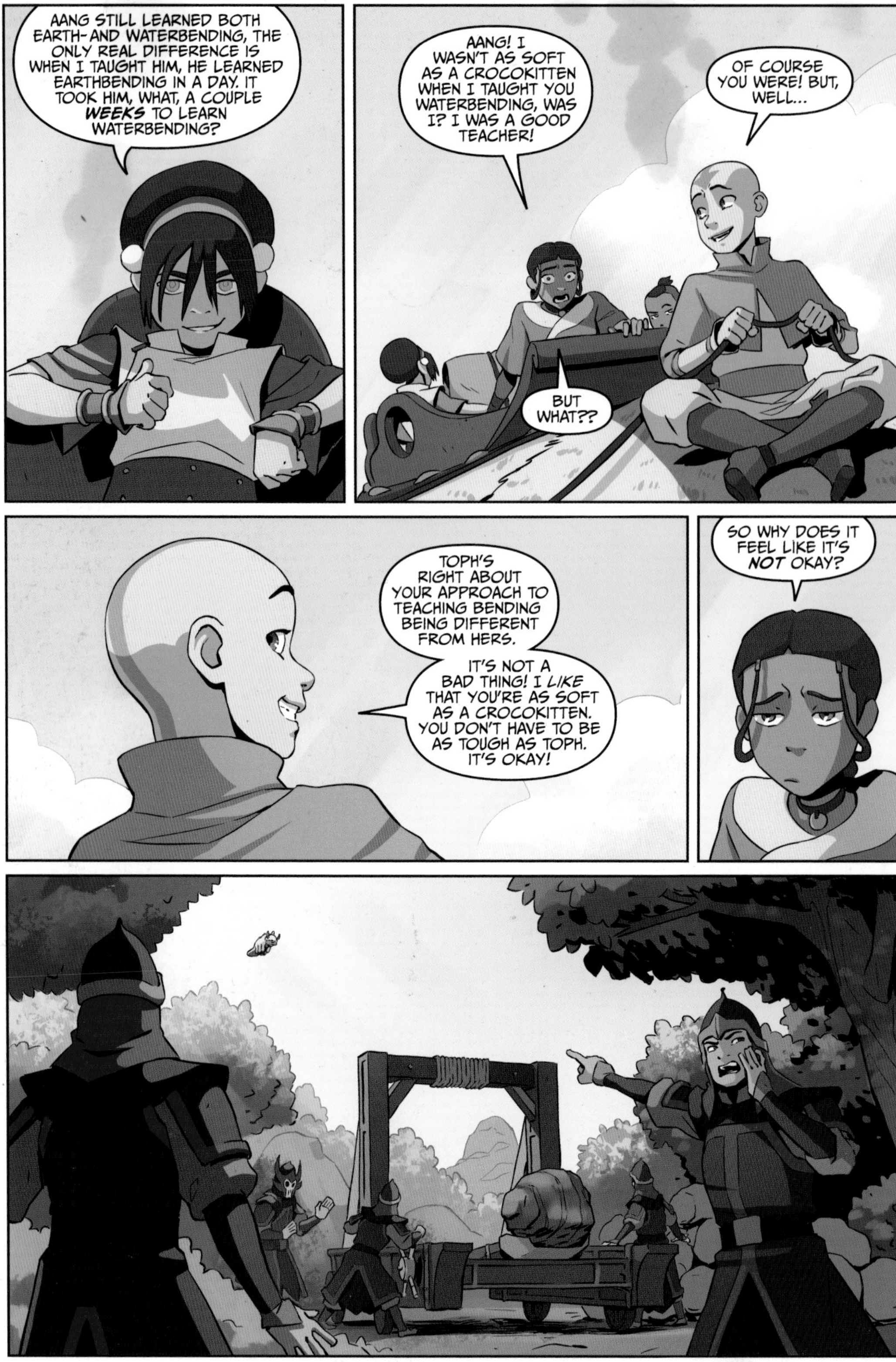
AANG STILL LEARNED BOTH EARTH- AND WATERBENDING, THE ONLY REAL DIFFERENCE IS WHEN I TAUGHT HIM, HE LEARNED EARTHBENDING IN A DAY. IT TOOK HIM, WHAT, A COUPLE WEEKS TO LEARN WATERBENDING?
AANG! I WASN'T AS SOFT AS A CROCOKITTEN WHEN I TAUGHT YOU WATERBENDING, WAS I? I WAS A GOOD TEACHER!
OF COURSE YOU WERE! BUT, WELL...
BUT WHAT??
TOPH'S RIGHT ABOUT YOUR APPROACH TO TEACHING BENDING BEING DIFFERENT FROM HERS.
IT'S NOT A BAD THING! I LIKE THAT YOU'RE AS SOFT AS A CROCOKITTEN. YOU DON'T HAVE TO BE AS TOUGH AS TOPH. IT'S OKAY!
SO WHY DOES IT FEEL LIKE IT'S NOT OKAY?

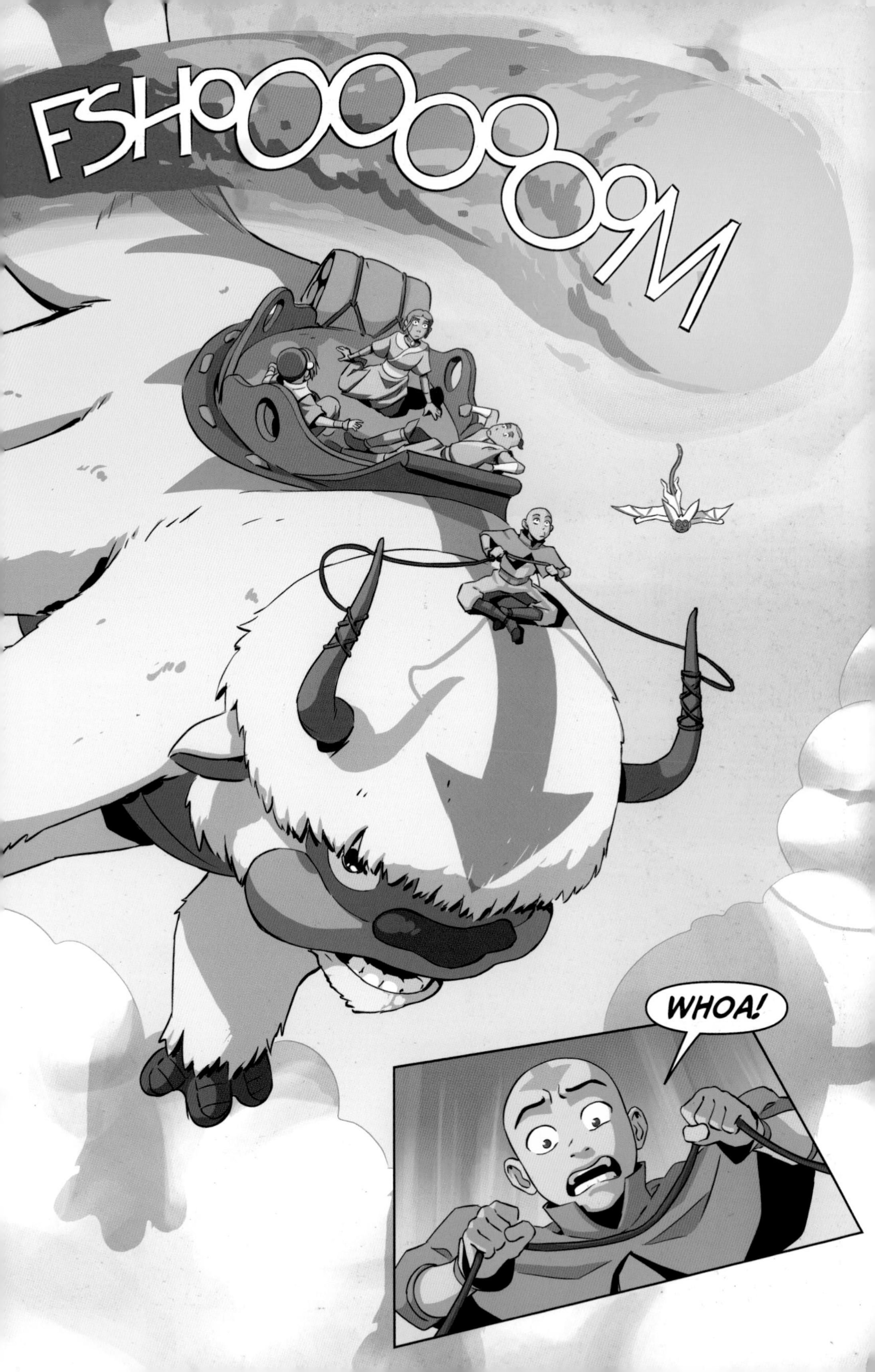
FSHOOOOOOM
WHOA!

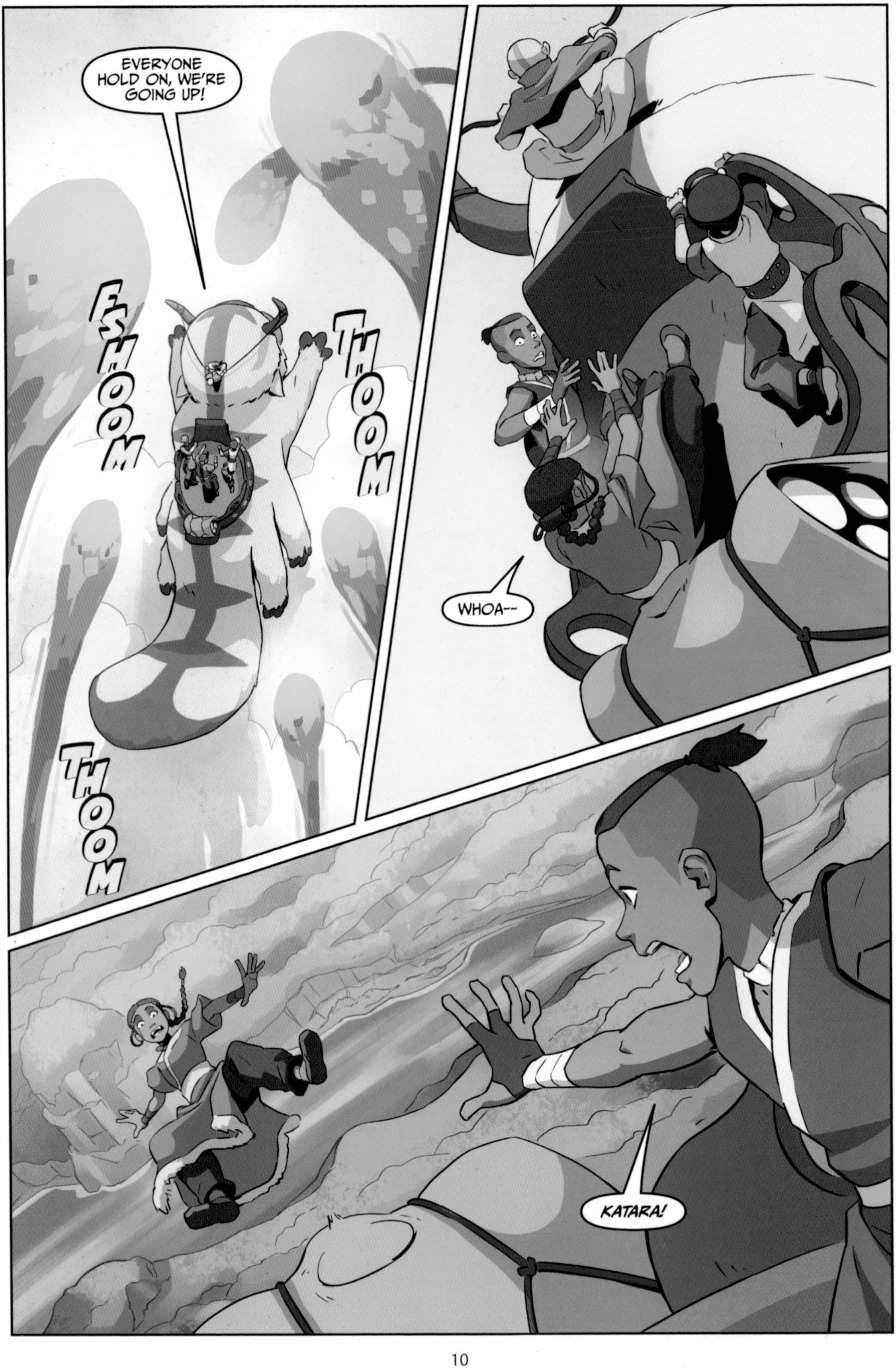
EVERYONE HOLD ON, WE'RE GOING UP!
FSHOOM
THOOM
THOOM
WHOA--
KATARA!

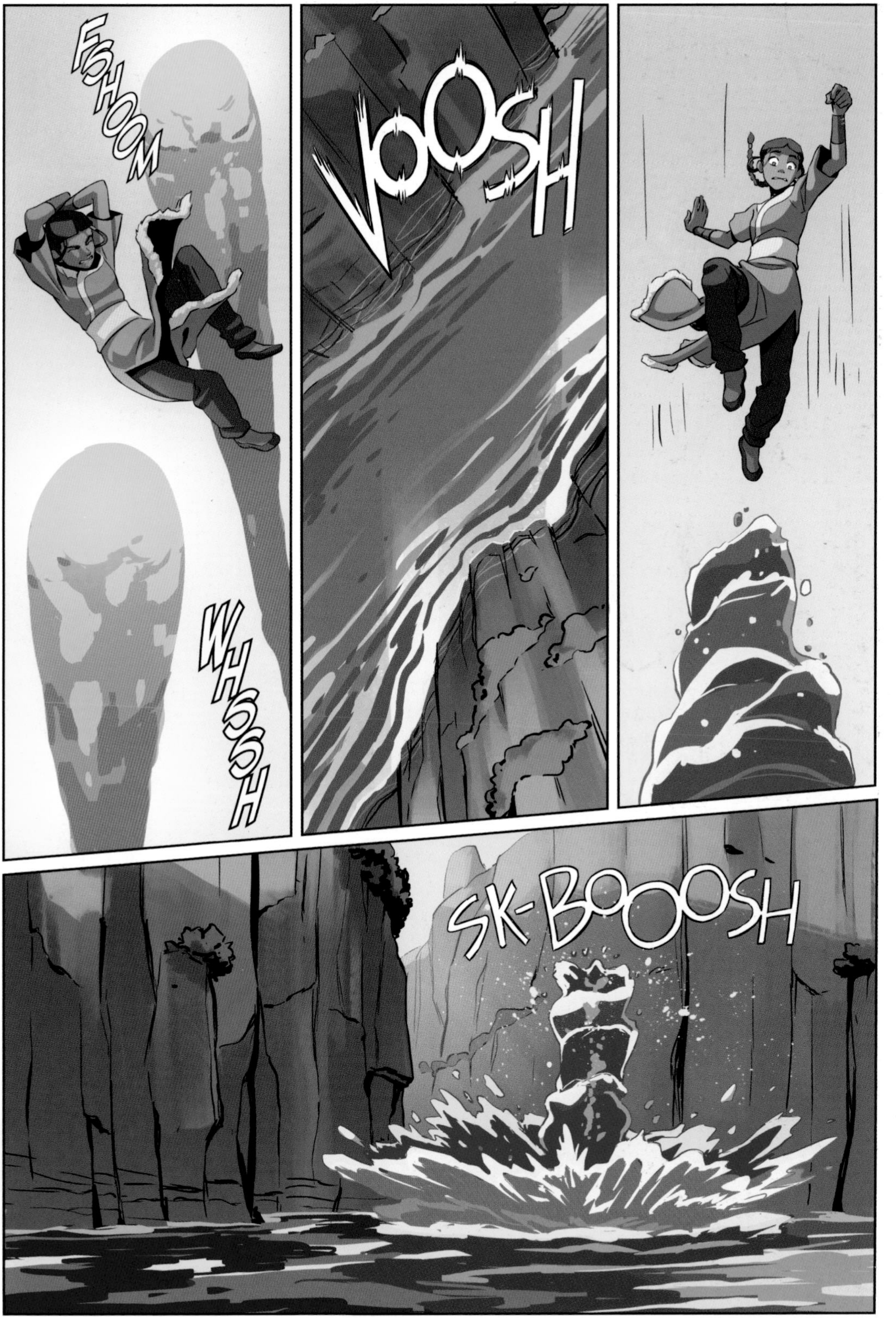
FSHOOM
WHOOSH
VOOSH
SK-BOOOSH

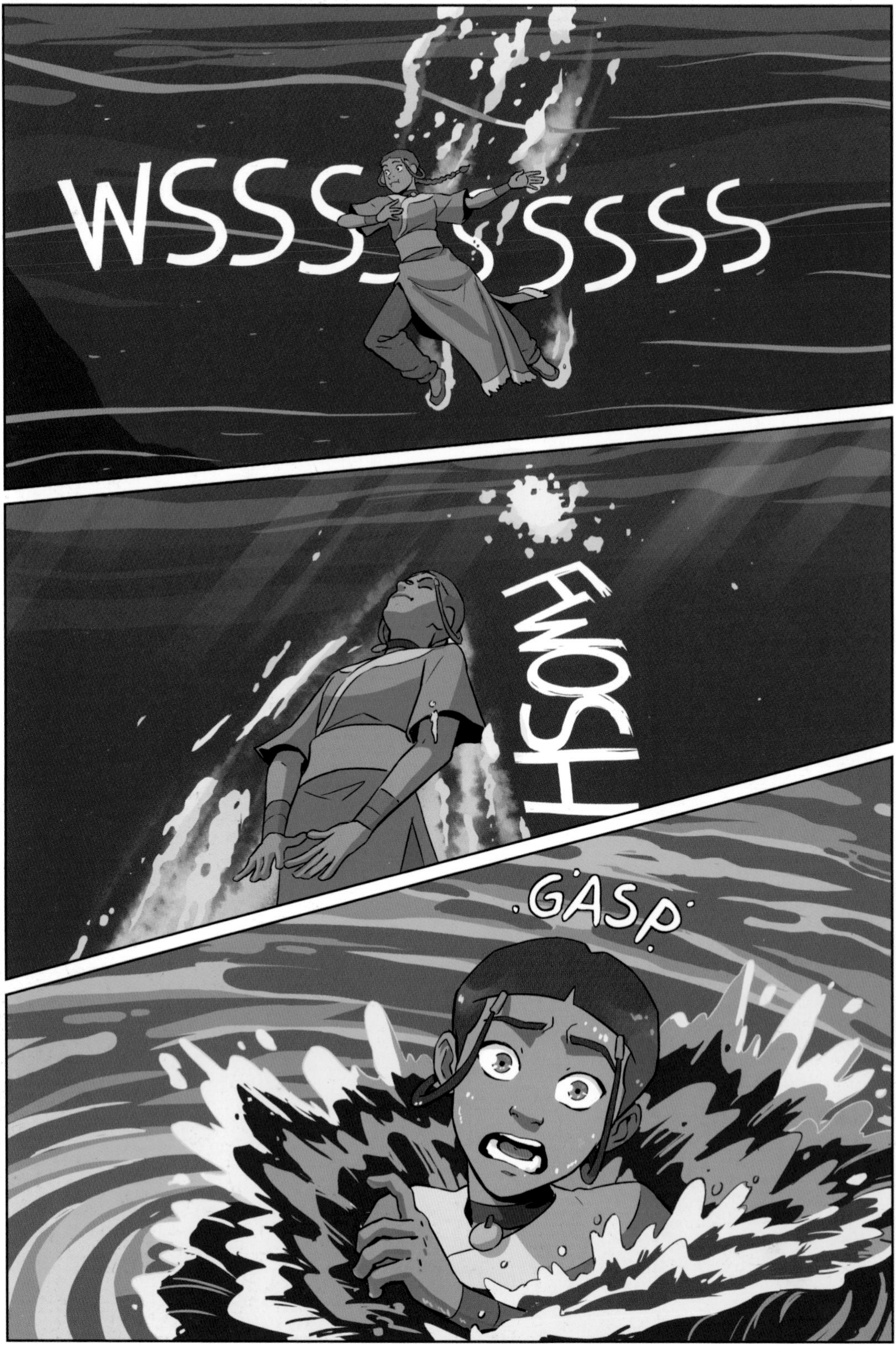
WSSSSSSSSS
FWOSH
GASP

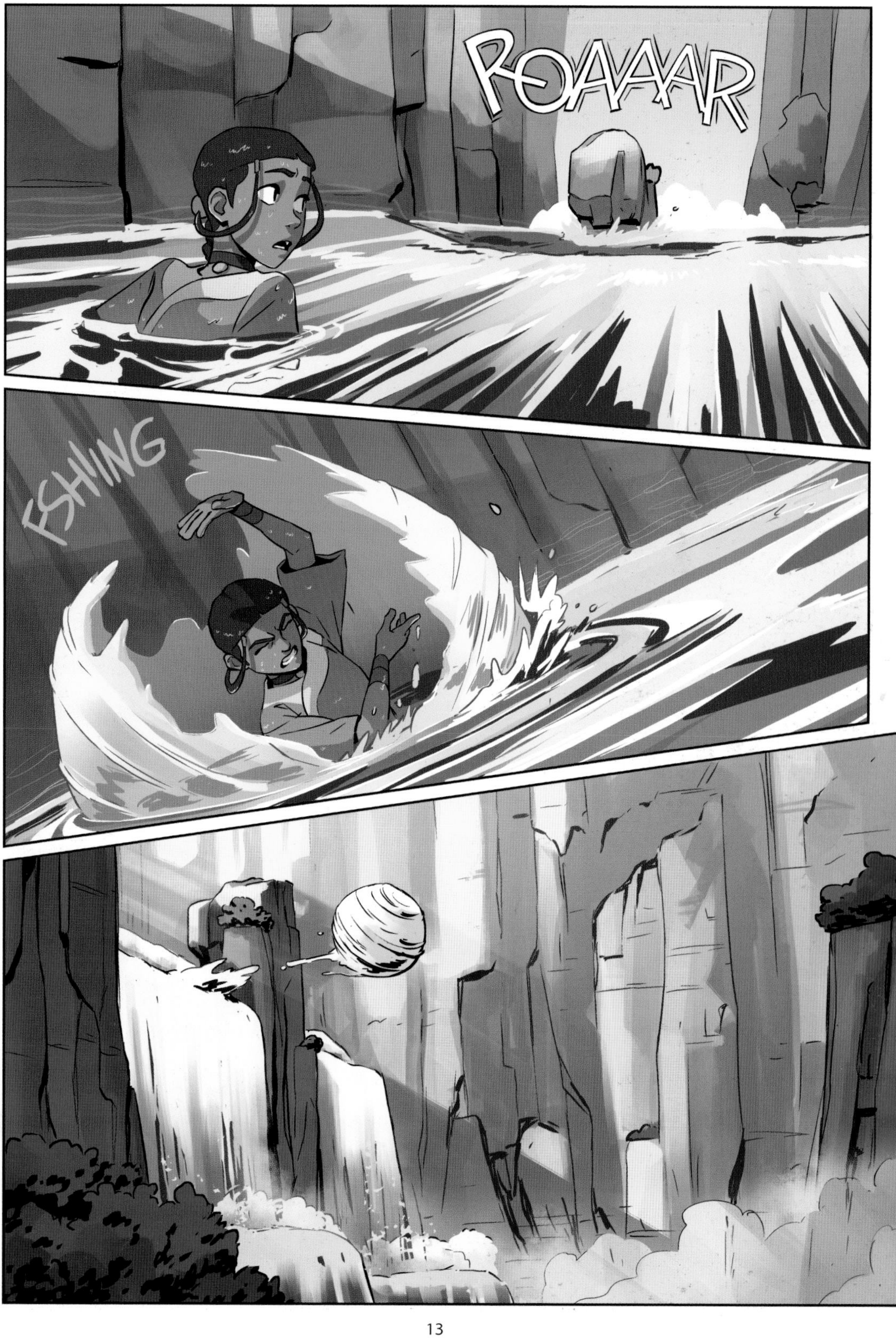
ROAAAR
FSHING

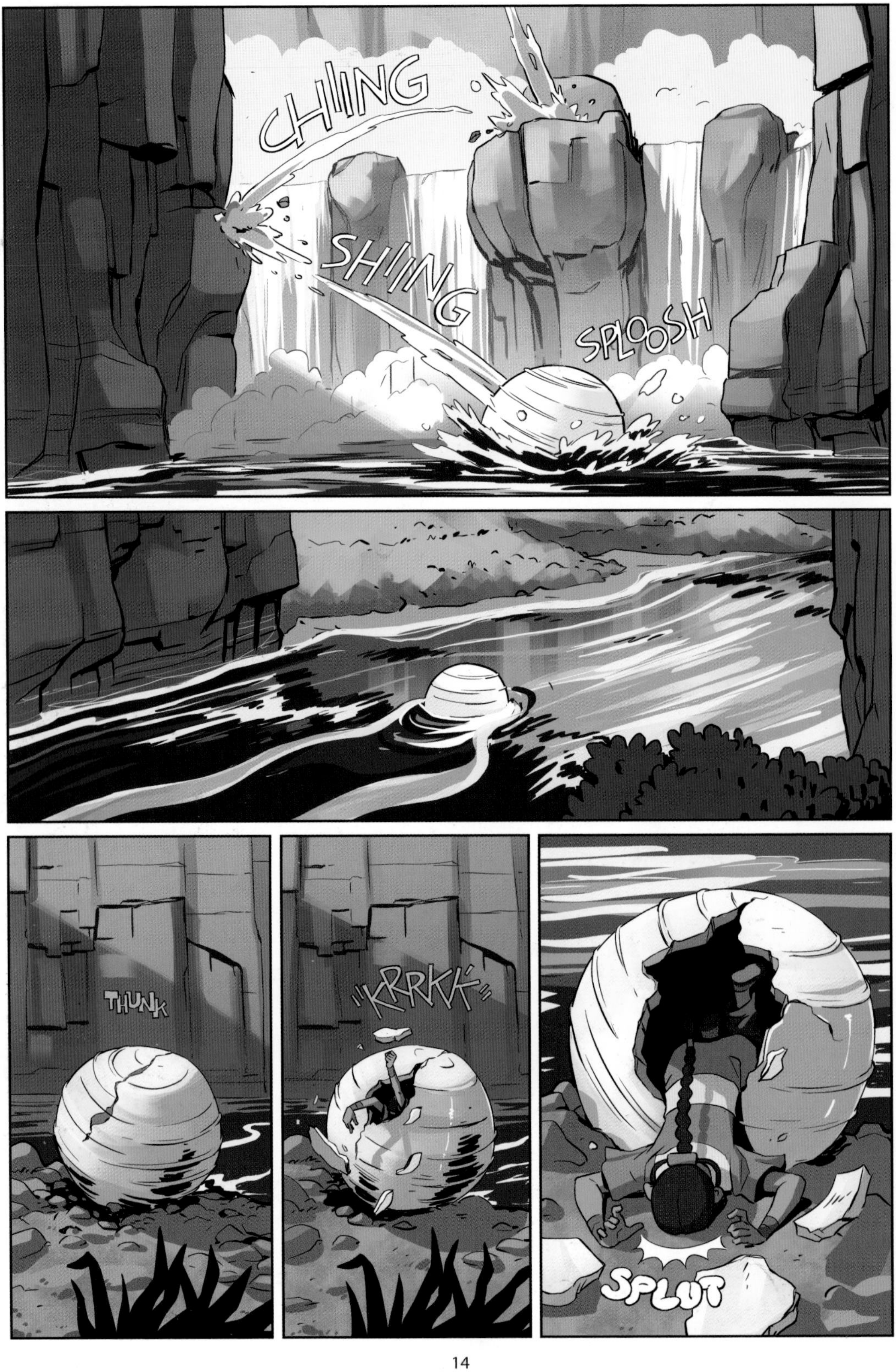
CHIING
SHIING
SPLOOSH
THUNK
"KRRKK"
SPLUT

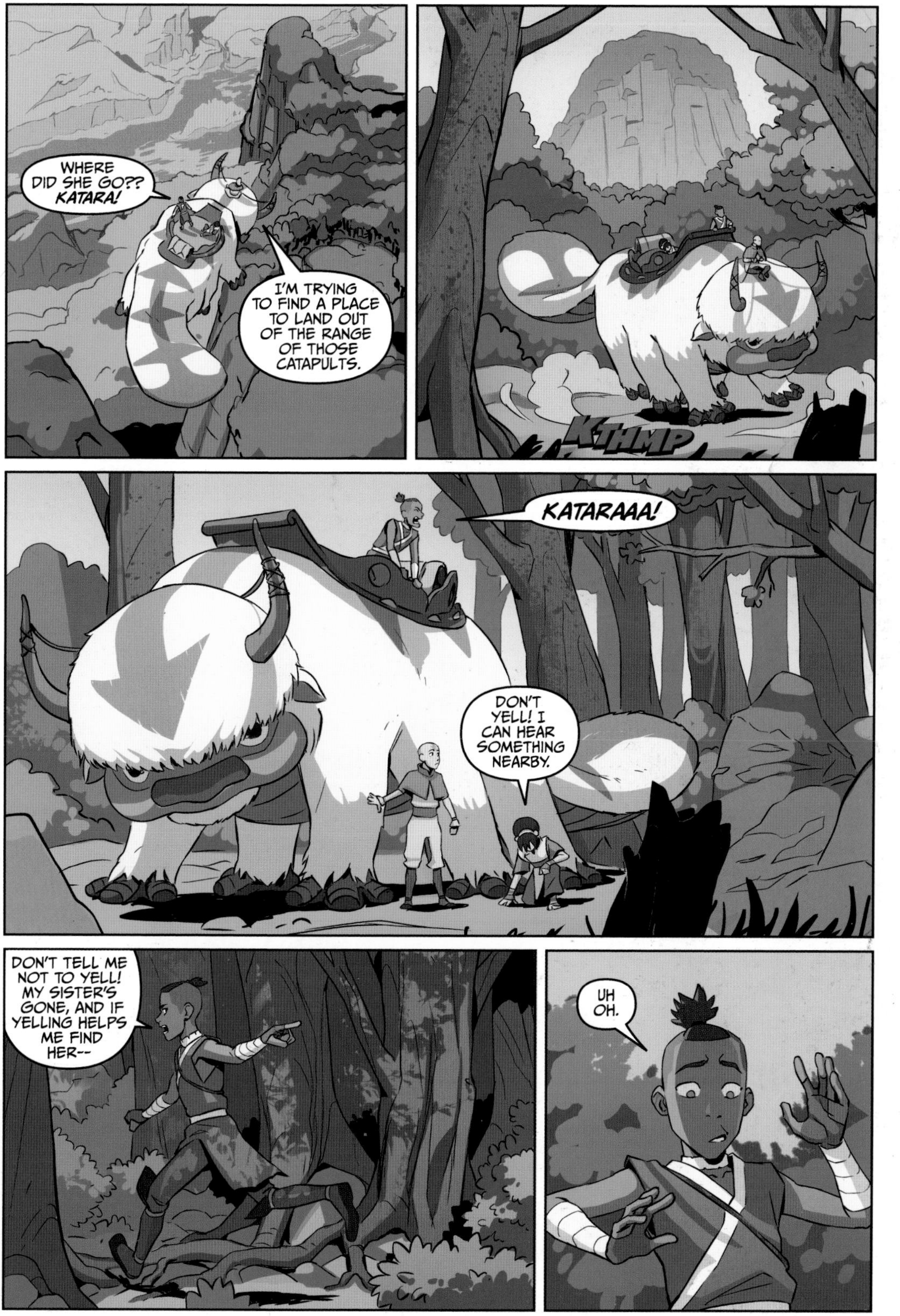
WHERE DID SHE GO?? KATARA!
I'M TRYING TO FIND A PLACE TO LAND OUT OF THE RANGE OF THOSE CATAPULTS.
KTHMP
KATARAAA!
DON'T YELL! I CAN HEAR SOMETHING NEARBY.
DON'T TELL ME NOT TO YELL! MY SISTER'S GONE, AND IF YELLING HELPS ME FIND HER--
UH OH.

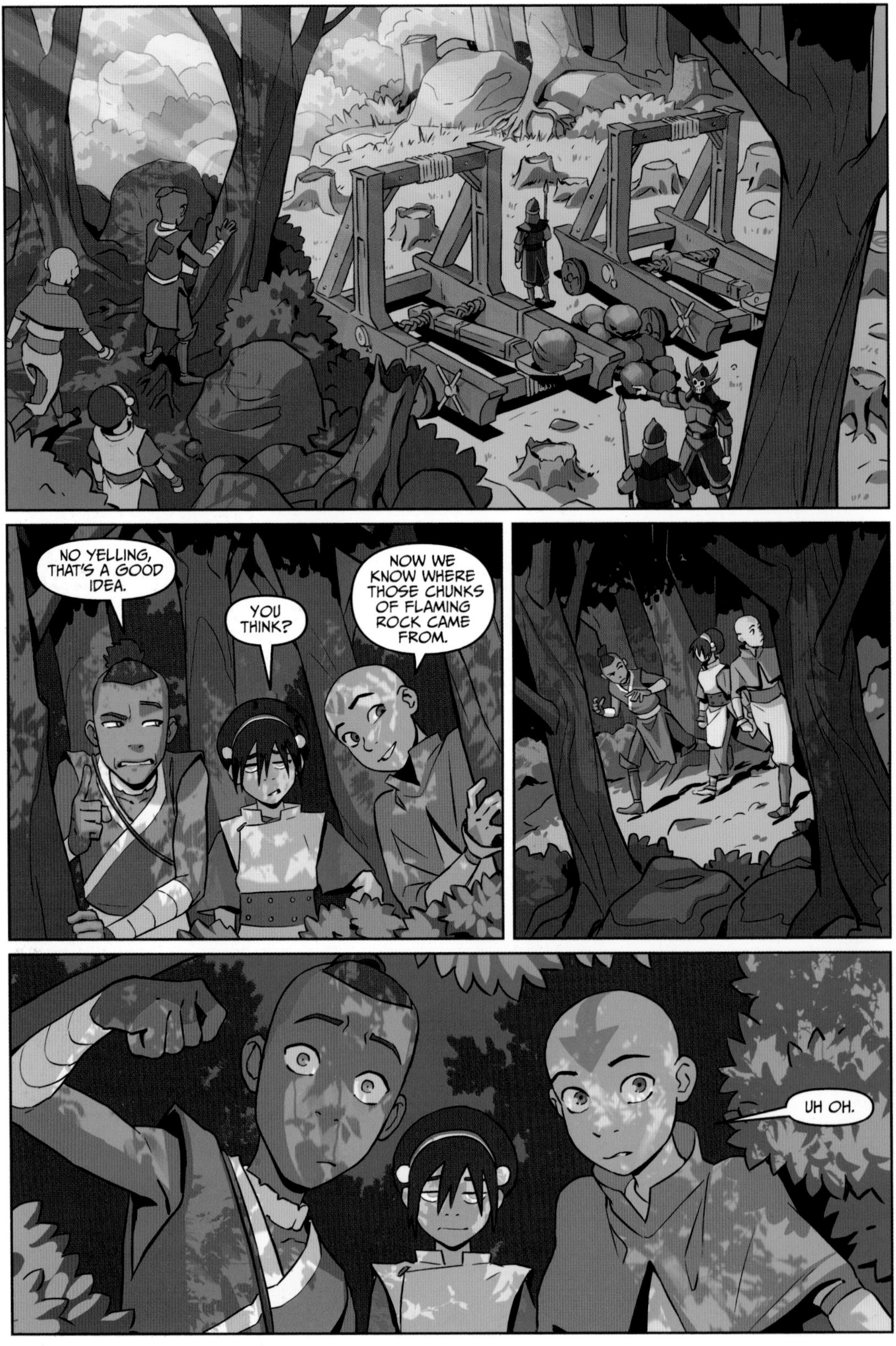
NO YELLING, THAT'S A GOOD IDEA.
YOU THINK?
NOW WE KNOW WHERE THOSE CHUNKS OF FLAMING ROCK CAME FROM.
UH OH.

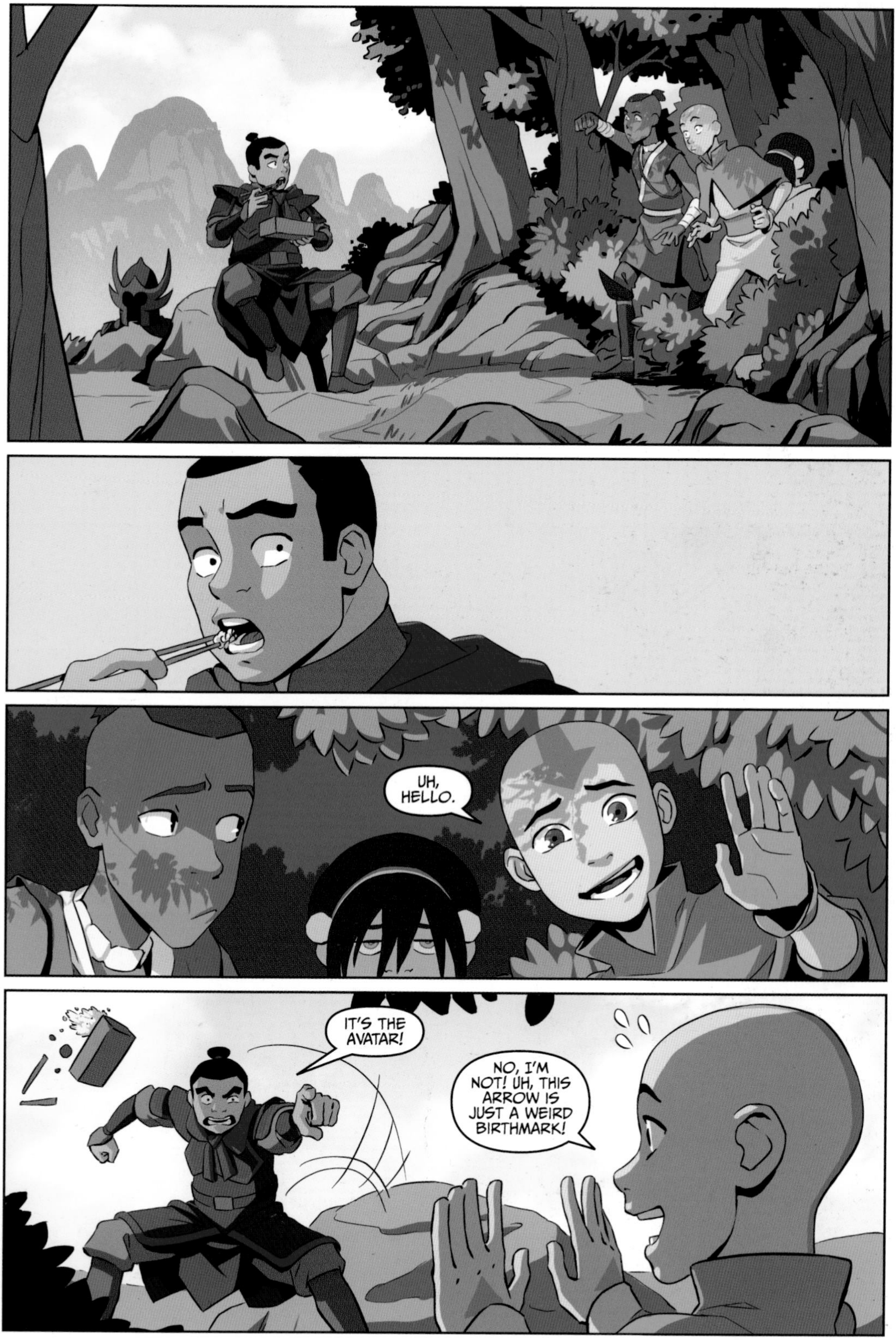
UH, HELLO.
IT'S THE AVATAR!
NO, I'M NOT! UH, THIS ARROW IS JUST A WEIRD BIRTHMARK!

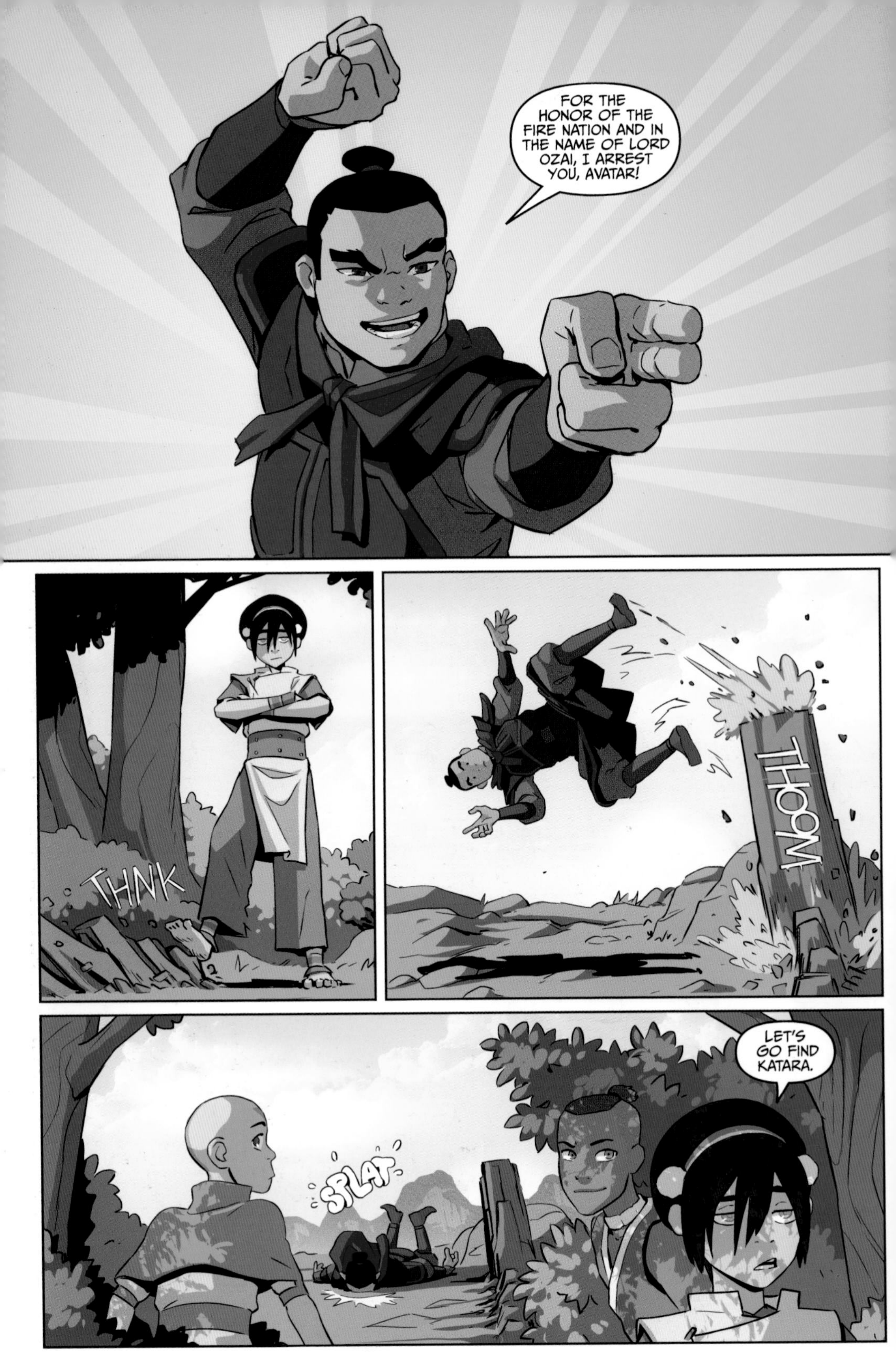
FOR THE HONOR OF THE FIRE NATION AND IN THE NAME OF LORD OZAI, I ARREST YOU, AVATAR!
THNK
THOOM!
SPLAT
LET'S GO FIND KATARA.

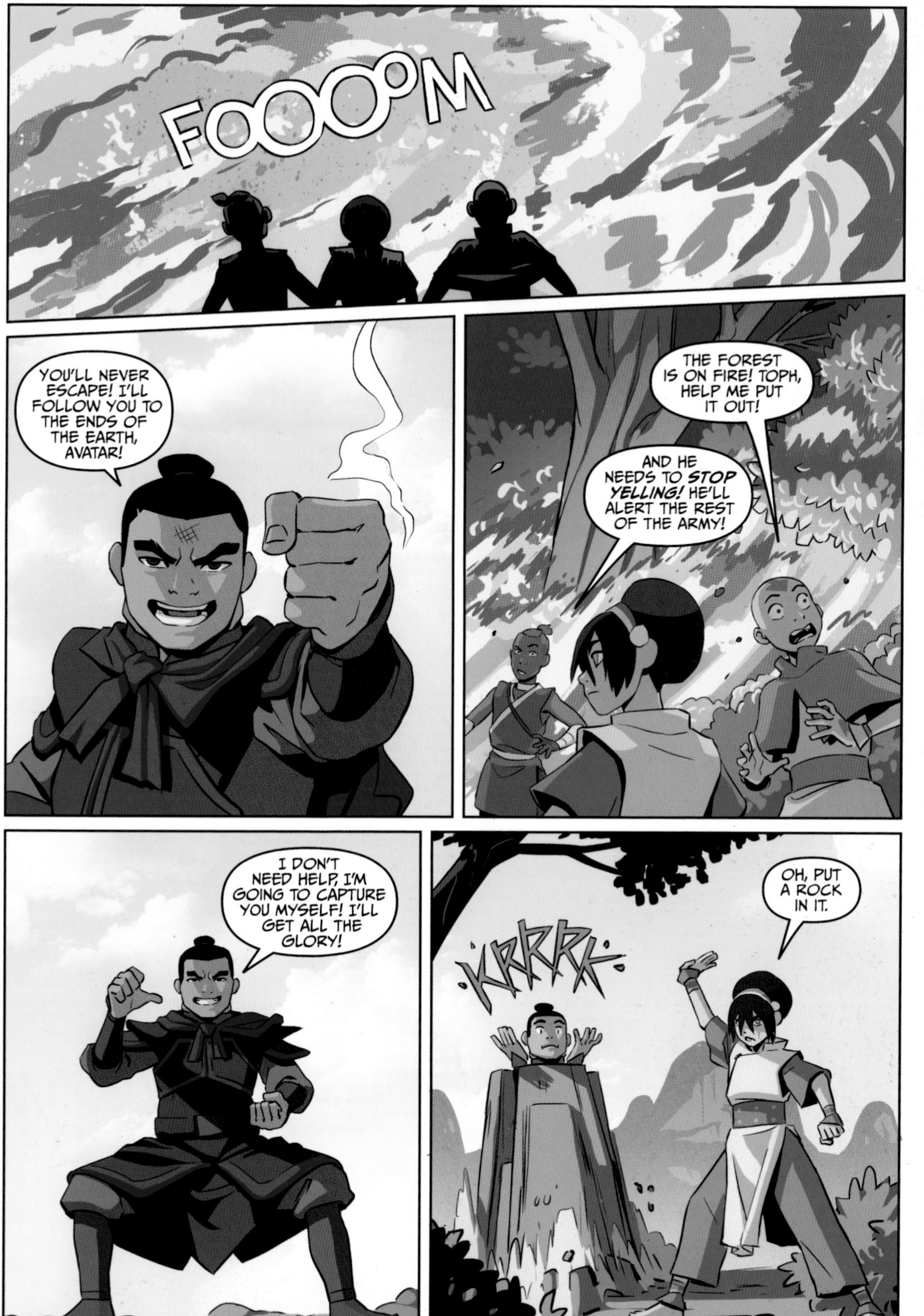
FOOOOM
YOU'LL NEVER ESCAPE! I'LL FOLLOW YOU TO THE ENDS OF THE EARTH, AVATAR!
THE FOREST IS ON FIRE! TOPH, HELP ME PUT IT OUT!
AND HE NEEDS TO STOP YELLING! HE'LL ALERT THE REST OF THE ARMY!
I DON'T NEED HELP, I'M GOING TO CAPTURE YOU MYSELF! I'LL GET ALL THE GLORY!
OH, PUT A ROCK IN IT.
KRRRK

DOOF

OKAY, FIRE'S OUT. *NOW* CAN WE GO FIND MY SISTER?

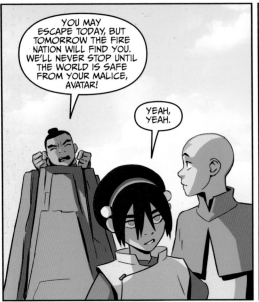

YOU MAY ESCAPE TODAY, BUT TOMORROW THE FIRE NATION WILL FIND YOU. WE'LL NEVER STOP UNTIL THE WORLD IS SAFE FROM YOUR MALICE, AVATAR!

YEAH, YEAH.

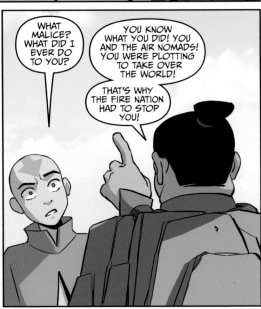

WHAT MALICE? WHAT DID I EVER DO TO YOU?

YOU KNOW WHAT YOU DID! YOU AND THE AIR NOMADS! YOU WERE PLOTTING TO TAKE OVER THE WORLD!

THAT'S WHY THE FIRE NATION HAD TO STOP YOU!

YOU *CAN'T* BELIEVE THAT!

IT'S THE TRUTH!

IT'S A *LIE!*

SO PROVE IT.

20

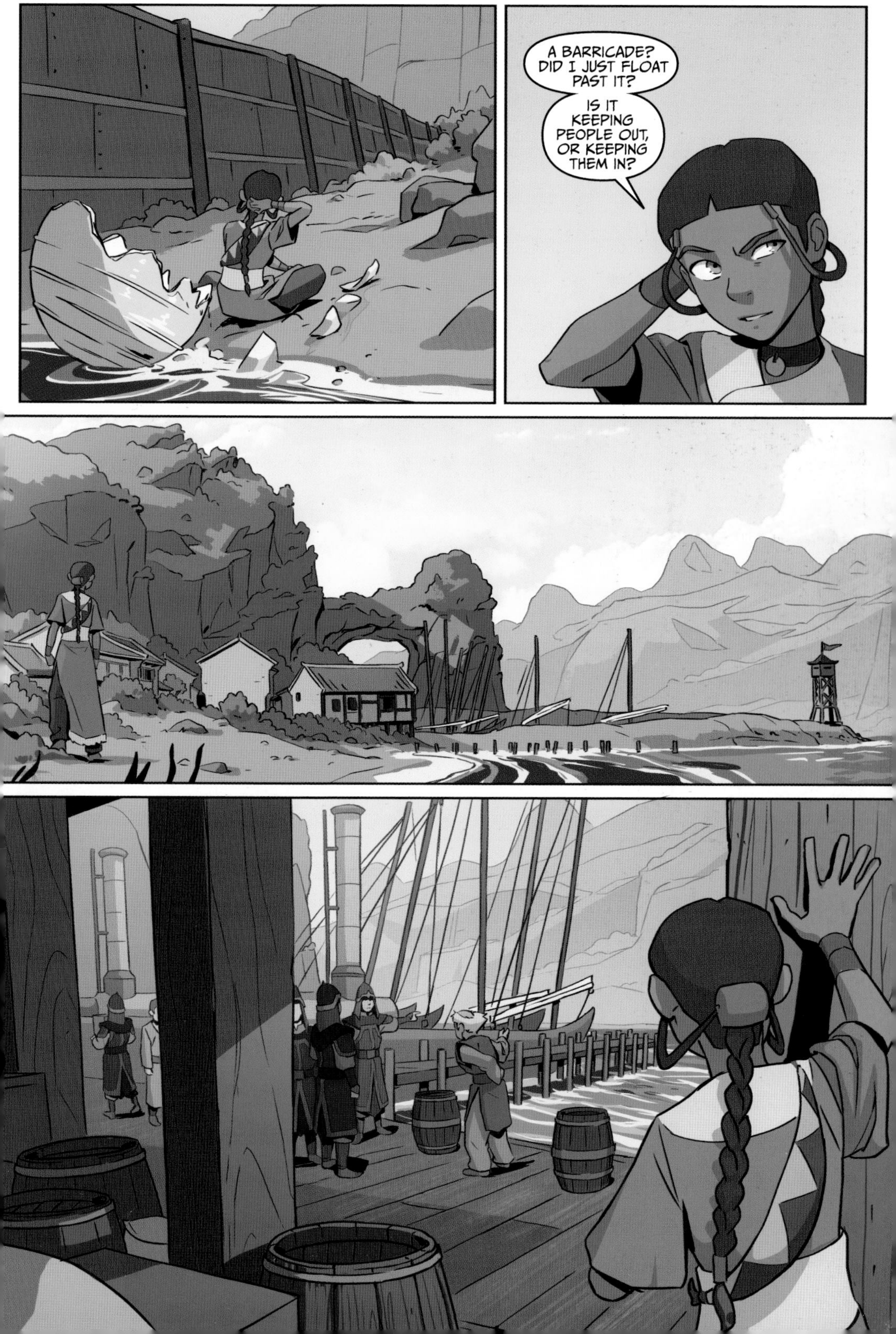
A BARRICADE? DID I JUST FLOAT PAST IT?
IS IT KEEPING PEOPLE OUT, OR KEEPING THEM IN?

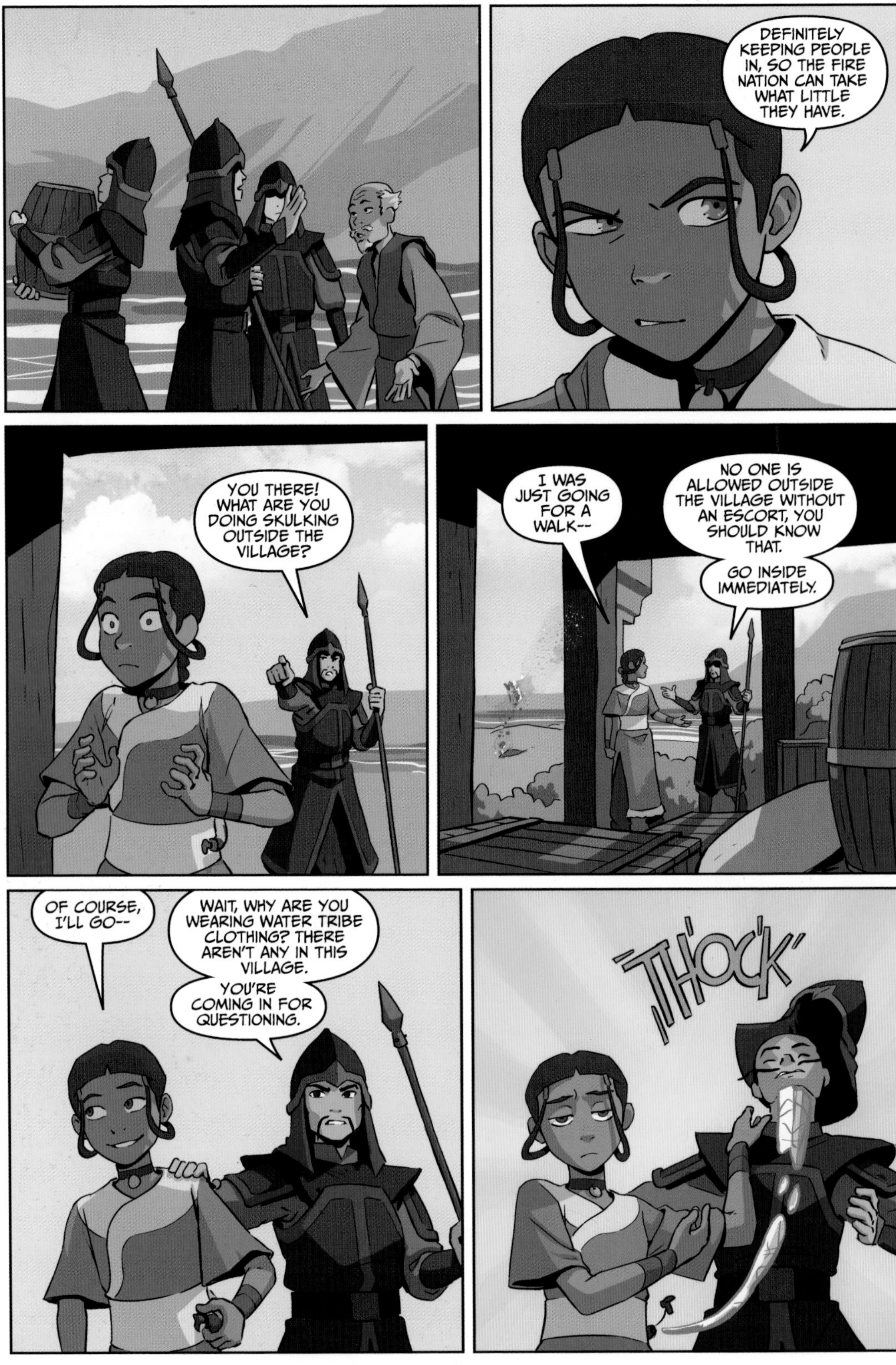
DEFINITELY KEEPING PEOPLE IN, SO THE FIRE NATION CAN TAKE WHAT LITTLE THEY HAVE.
YOU THERE! WHAT ARE YOU DOING SKULKING OUTSIDE THE VILLAGE?
I WAS JUST GOING FOR A WALK--
NO ONE IS ALLOWED OUTSIDE THE VILLAGE WITHOUT AN ESCORT, YOU SHOULD KNOW THAT.
GO INSIDE IMMEDIATELY.
OF COURSE, I'LL GO--
WAIT, WHY ARE YOU WEARING WATER TRIBE CLOTHING? THERE AREN'T ANY IN THIS VILLAGE.
YOU'RE COMING IN FOR QUESTIONING.
THOCK

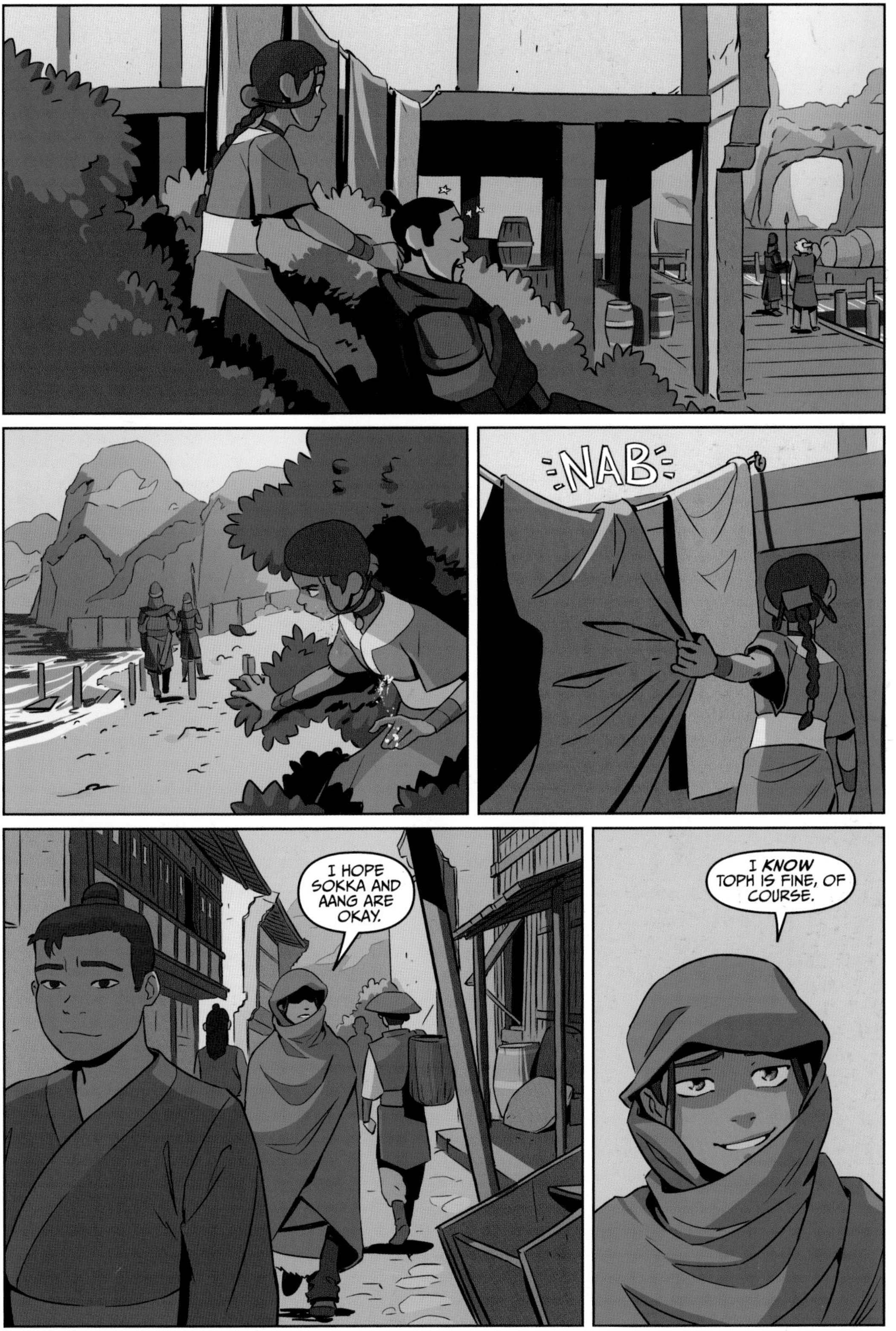
NAB
I HOPE SOKKA AND AANG ARE OKAY.
I KNOW TOPH IS FINE, OF COURSE.

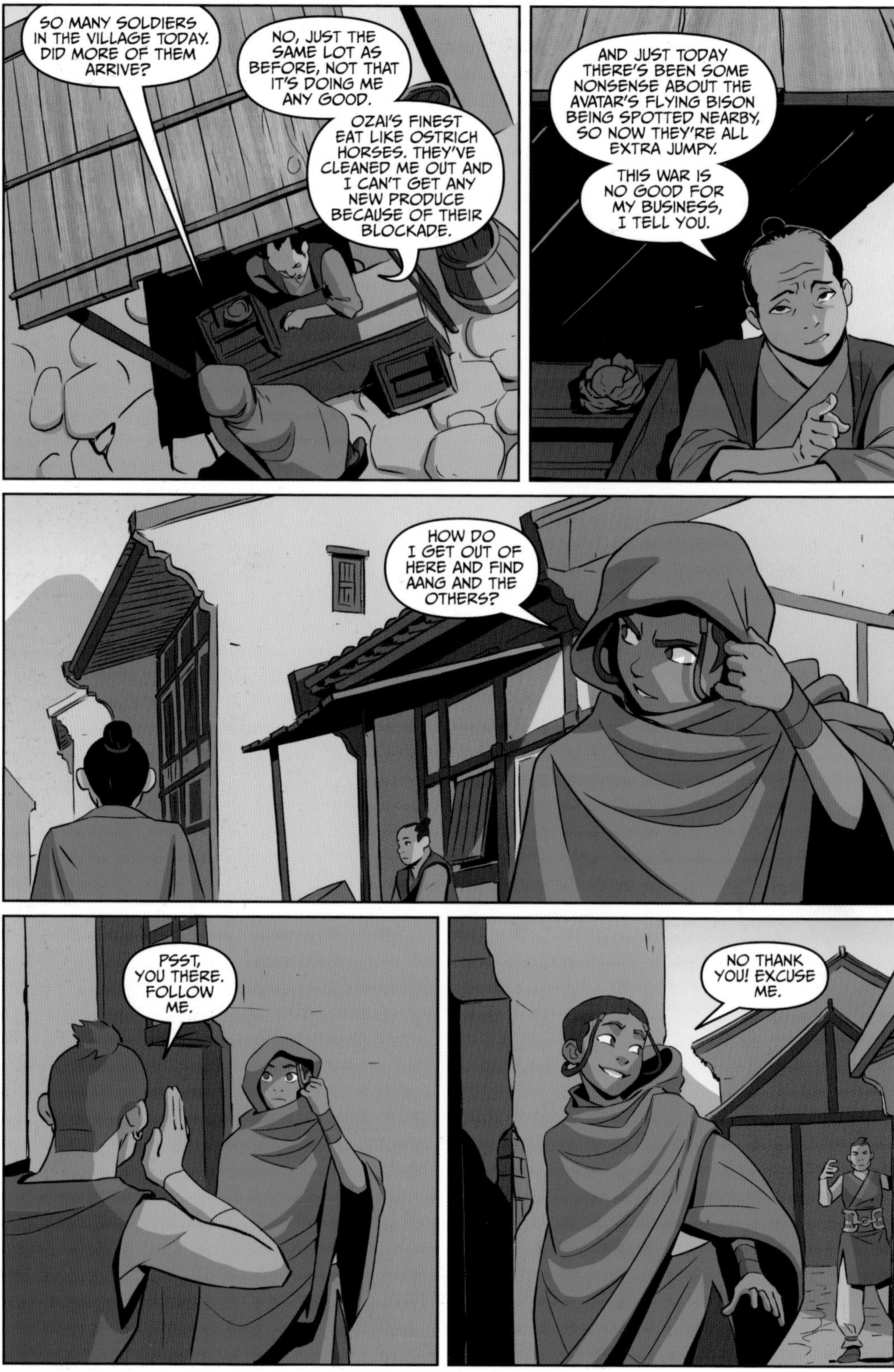
SO MANY SOLDIERS IN THE VILLAGE TODAY. DID MORE OF THEM ARRIVE?
NO, JUST THE SAME LOT AS BEFORE, NOT THAT IT'S DOING ME ANY GOOD.
OZAI'S FINEST EAT LIKE OSTRICH HORSES. THEY'VE CLEANED ME OUT AND I CAN'T GET ANY NEW PRODUCE BECAUSE OF THEIR BLOCKADE.
AND JUST TODAY THERE'S BEEN SOME NONSENSE ABOUT THE AVATAR'S FLYING BISON BEING SPOTTED NEARBY, SO NOW THEY'RE ALL EXTRA JUMPY.
THIS WAR IS NO GOOD FOR MY BUSINESS, I TELL YOU.
HOW DO I GET OUT OF HERE AND FIND AANG AND THE OTHERS?
PSST, YOU THERE. FOLLOW ME.
NO THANK YOU! EXCUSE ME.

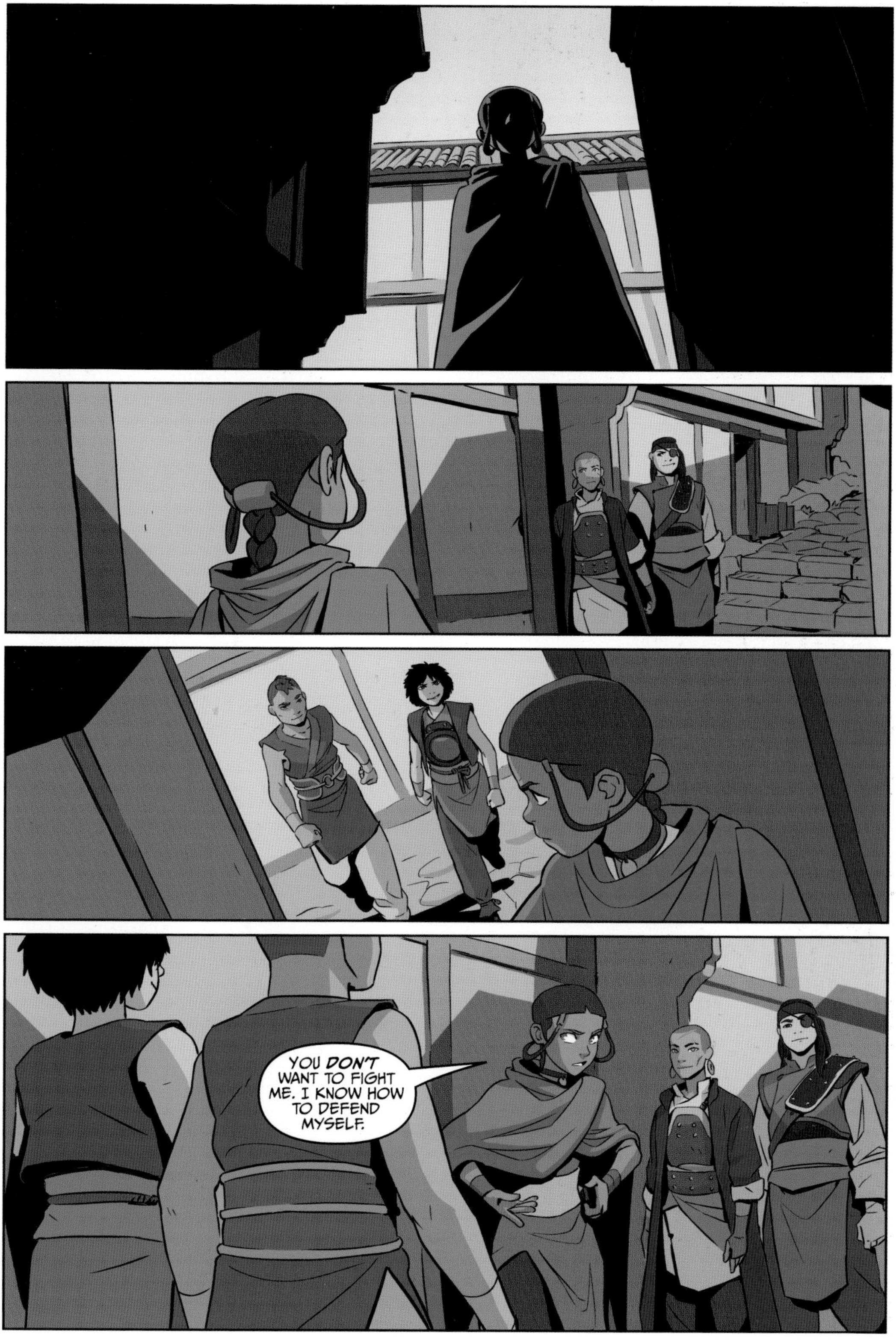
YOU DON'T WANT TO FIGHT ME. I KNOW HOW TO DEFEND MYSELF.

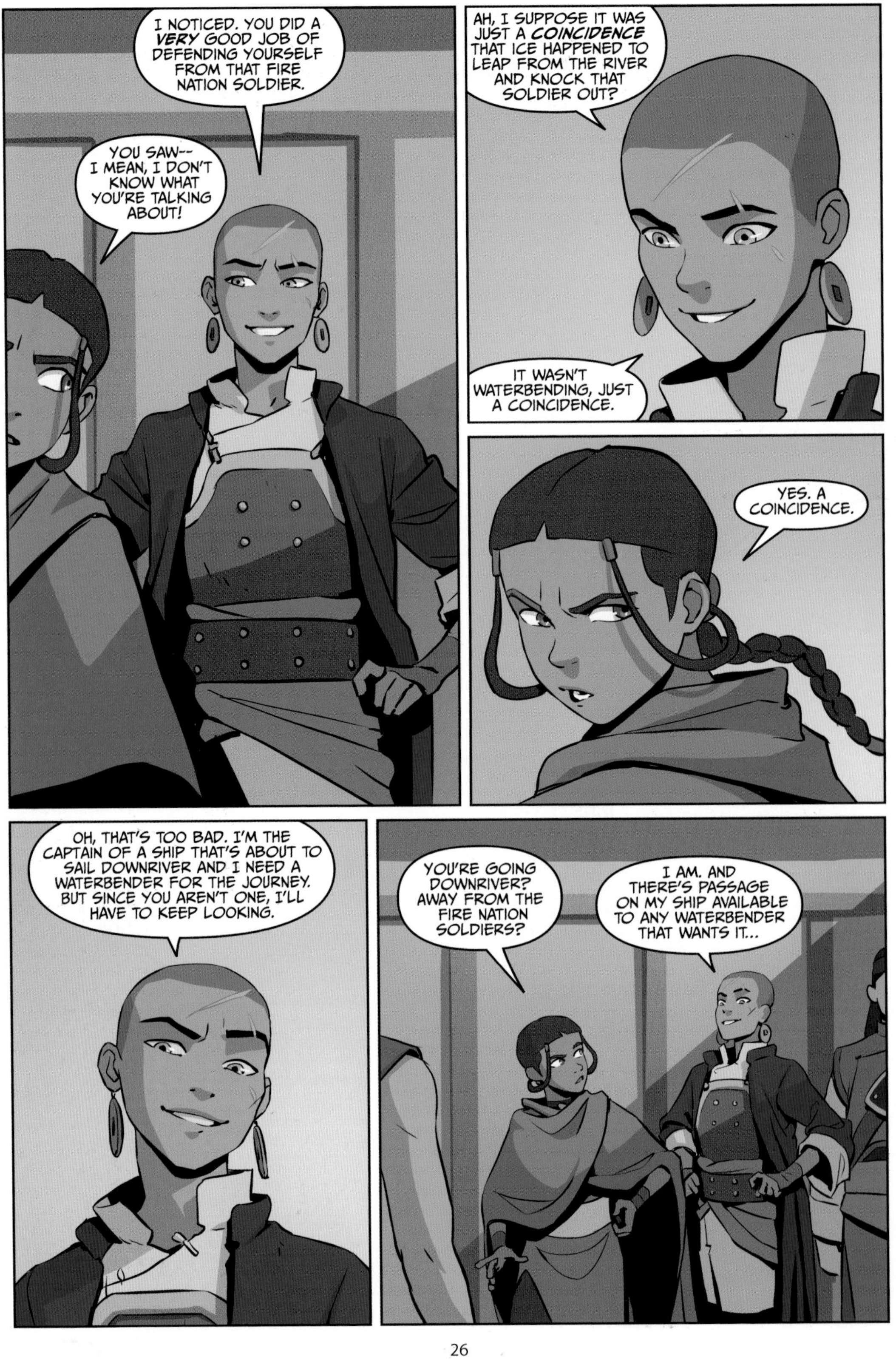
I NOTICED. YOU DID A VERY GOOD JOB OF DEFENDING YOURSELF FROM THAT FIRE NATION SOLDIER.
YOU SAW-- I MEAN, I DON'T KNOW WHAT YOU'RE TALKING ABOUT!
AH, I SUPPOSE IT WAS JUST A COINCIDENCE THAT ICE HAPPENED TO LEAP FROM THE RIVER AND KNOCK THAT SOLDIER OUT?
IT WASN'T WATERBENDING, JUST A COINCIDENCE.
YES. A COINCIDENCE.
OH, THAT'S TOO BAD. I'M THE CAPTAIN OF A SHIP THAT'S ABOUT TO SAIL DOWNRIVER AND I NEED A WATERBENDER FOR THE JOURNEY. BUT SINCE YOU AREN'T ONE, I'LL HAVE TO KEEP LOOKING.
YOU'RE GOING DOWNRIVER? AWAY FROM THE FIRE NATION SOLDIERS?
I AM. AND THERE'S PASSAGE ON MY SHIP AVAILABLE TO ANY WATERBENDER THAT WANTS IT...

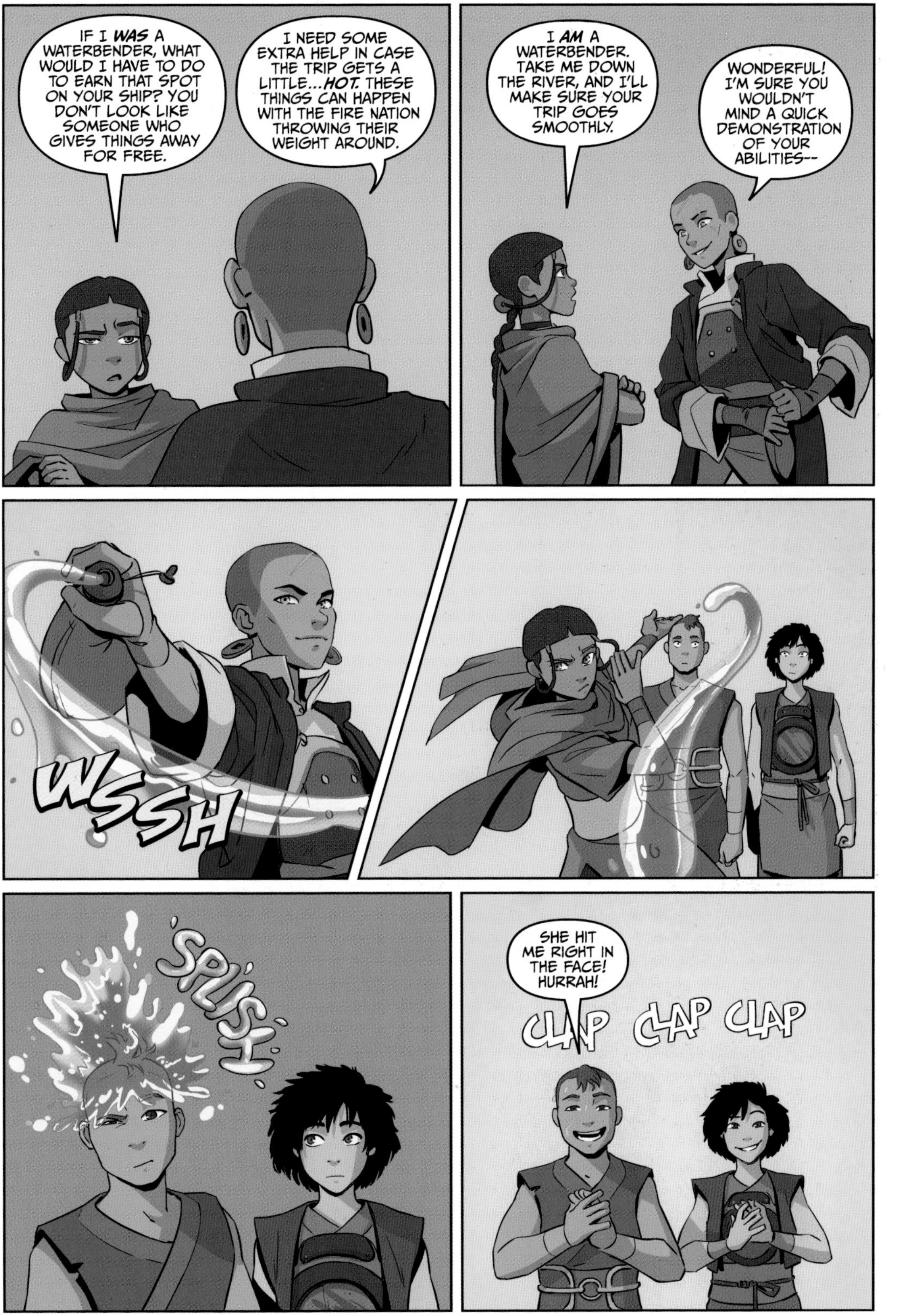
IF I WAS A WATERBENDER, WHAT WOULD I HAVE TO DO TO EARN THAT SPOT ON YOUR SHIP? YOU DON'T LOOK LIKE SOMEONE WHO GIVES THINGS AWAY FOR FREE.
I NEED SOME EXTRA HELP IN CASE THE TRIP GETS A LITTLE...HOT. THESE THINGS CAN HAPPEN WITH THE FIRE NATION THROWING THEIR WEIGHT AROUND.
I AM A WATERBENDER. TAKE ME DOWN THE RIVER, AND I'LL MAKE SURE YOUR TRIP GOES SMOOTHLY.
WONDERFUL! I'M SURE YOU WOULDN'T MIND A QUICK DEMONSTRATION OF YOUR ABILITIES--
WSSH
SPLISH
SHE HIT ME RIGHT IN THE FACE! HURRAH!
CLAP CLAP CLAP

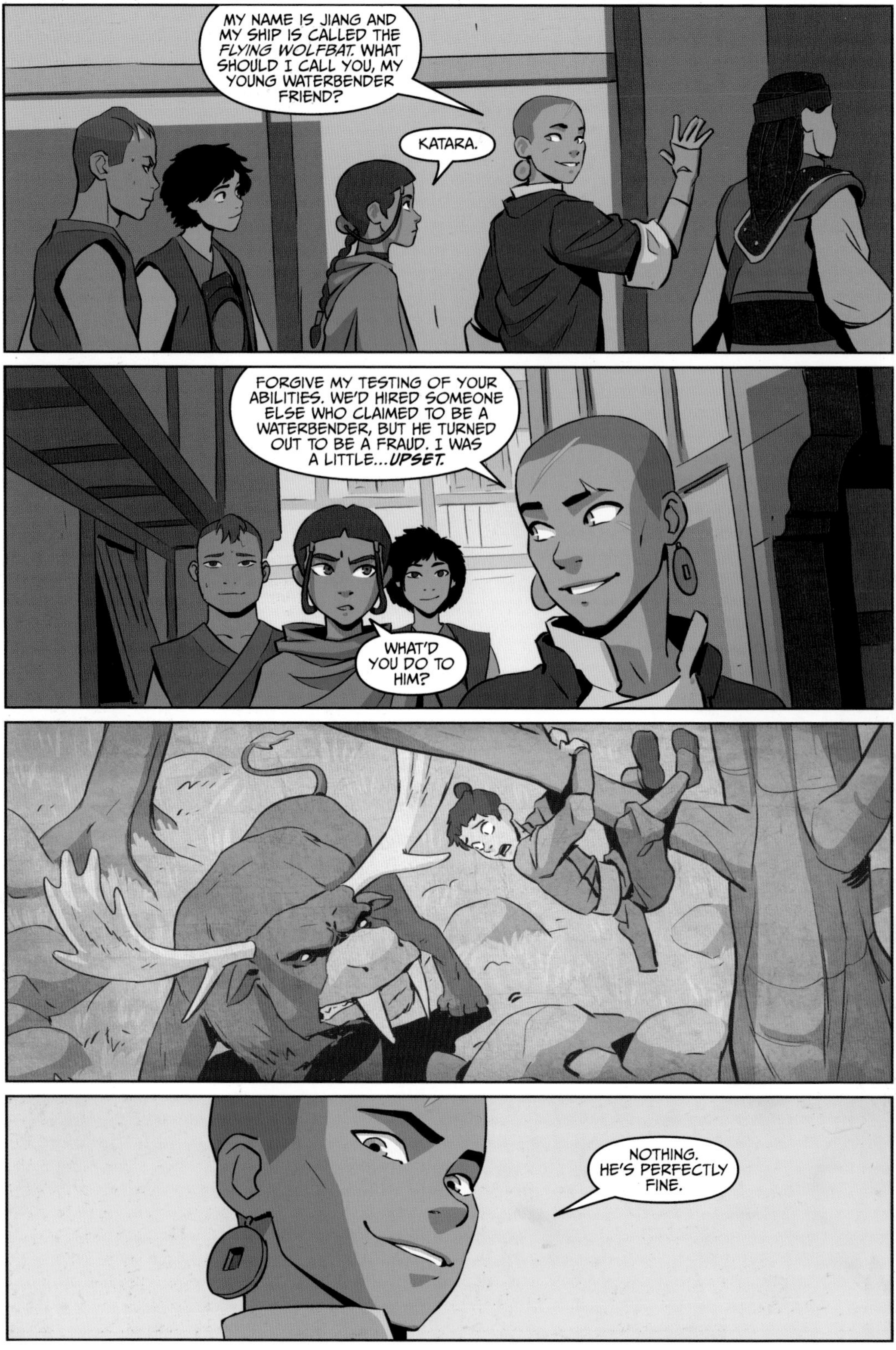
MY NAME IS JIANG AND MY SHIP IS CALLED THE *FLYING WOLFBAT.* WHAT SHOULD I CALL YOU, MY YOUNG WATERBENDER FRIEND?
KATARA.
FORGIVE MY TESTING OF YOUR ABILITIES. WE'D HIRED SOMEONE ELSE WHO CLAIMED TO BE A WATERBENDER, BUT HE TURNED OUT TO BE A FRAUD. I WAS A LITTLE...*UPSET.*
WHAT'D YOU DO TO HIM?
NOTHING. HE'S PERFECTLY FINE.

I WANT TO TALK TO HIM. I WANT TO SEE IF I CAN CHANGE HIS MIND.

WHY? HE'S A FIRE NATION SOLDIER. HE'D TURN US OVER TO HIS FIRE LORD WITHOUT A SECOND THOUGHT.

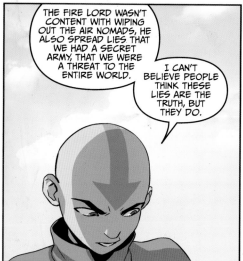

THE FIRE LORD WASN'T CONTENT WITH WIPING OUT THE AIR NOMADS, HE ALSO SPREAD LIES THAT WE HAD A SECRET ARMY, THAT WE WERE A THREAT TO THE ENTIRE WORLD.

I CAN'T BELIEVE PEOPLE THINK THESE LIES ARE THE TRUTH, BUT THEY DO.

HE DOES. I HAVE TO TELL HIM HE'S WRONG. EVEN IF I ONLY CHANGE ONE MIND IN THE FIRE NATION, ISN'T THAT WORTH DOING?

OF COURSE IT IS, BUT...

I KNOW. KATARA'S LOST, AND WE HAVE TO LOOK FOR HER. WE DON'T HAVE TIME FOR THIS, I KNOW.

NO, I WAS *GOING* TO SAY, "THIS GUY'S CLEARLY AN IDIOT, YOU SURE YOU WANT TO TRY TALKING TO HIM?"

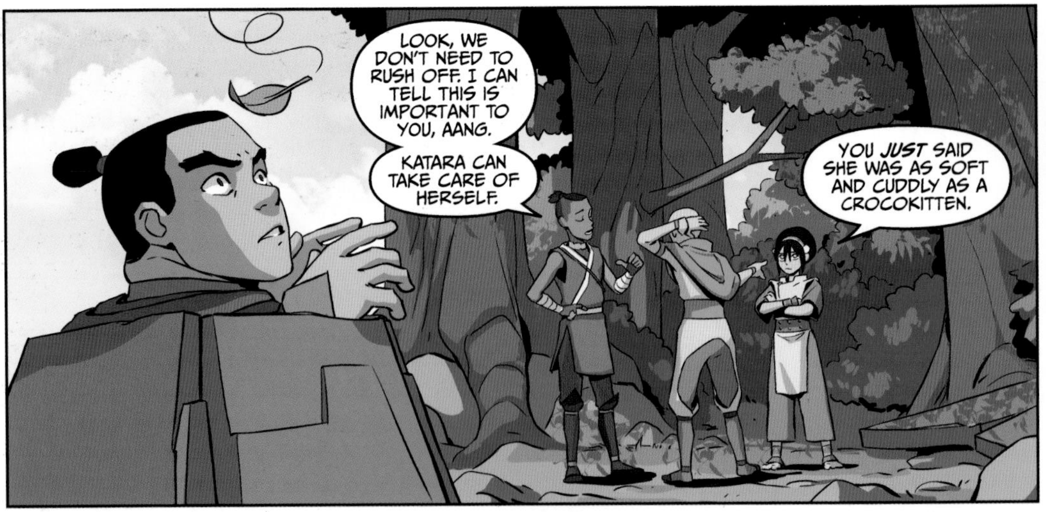
LOOK, WE DON'T NEED TO RUSH OFF. I CAN TELL THIS IS IMPORTANT TO YOU, AANG.
KATARA CAN TAKE CARE OF HERSELF.
YOU JUST SAID SHE WAS AS SOFT AND CUDDLY AS A CROCOKITTEN.

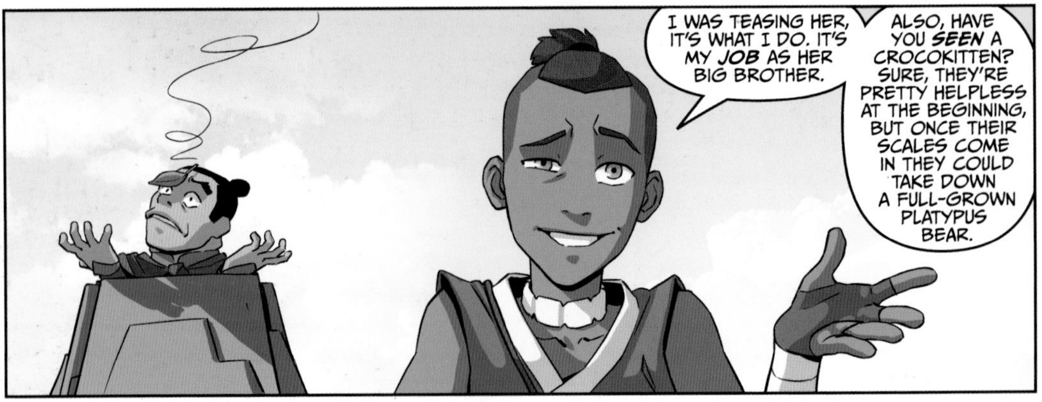
I WAS TEASING HER, IT'S WHAT I DO. IT'S MY JOB AS HER BIG BROTHER.
ALSO, HAVE YOU SEEN A CROCOKITTEN? SURE, THEY'RE PRETTY HELPLESS AT THE BEGINNING, BUT ONCE THEIR SCALES COME IN THEY COULD TAKE DOWN A FULL-GROWN PLATYPUS BEAR.

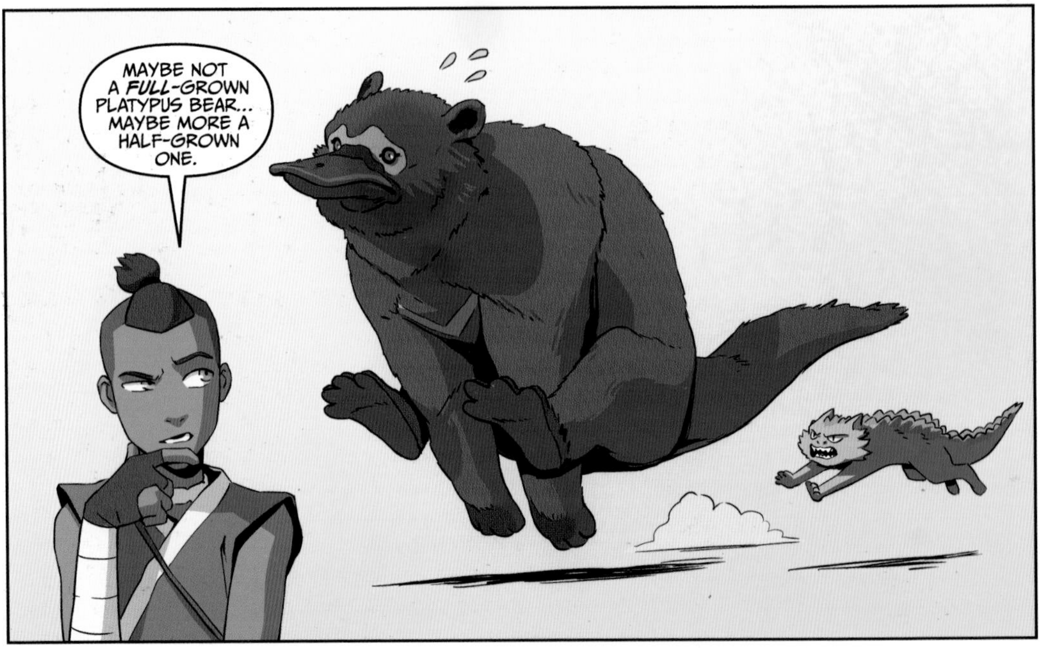
MAYBE NOT A FULL-GROWN PLATYPUS BEAR... MAYBE MORE A HALF-GROWN ONE.

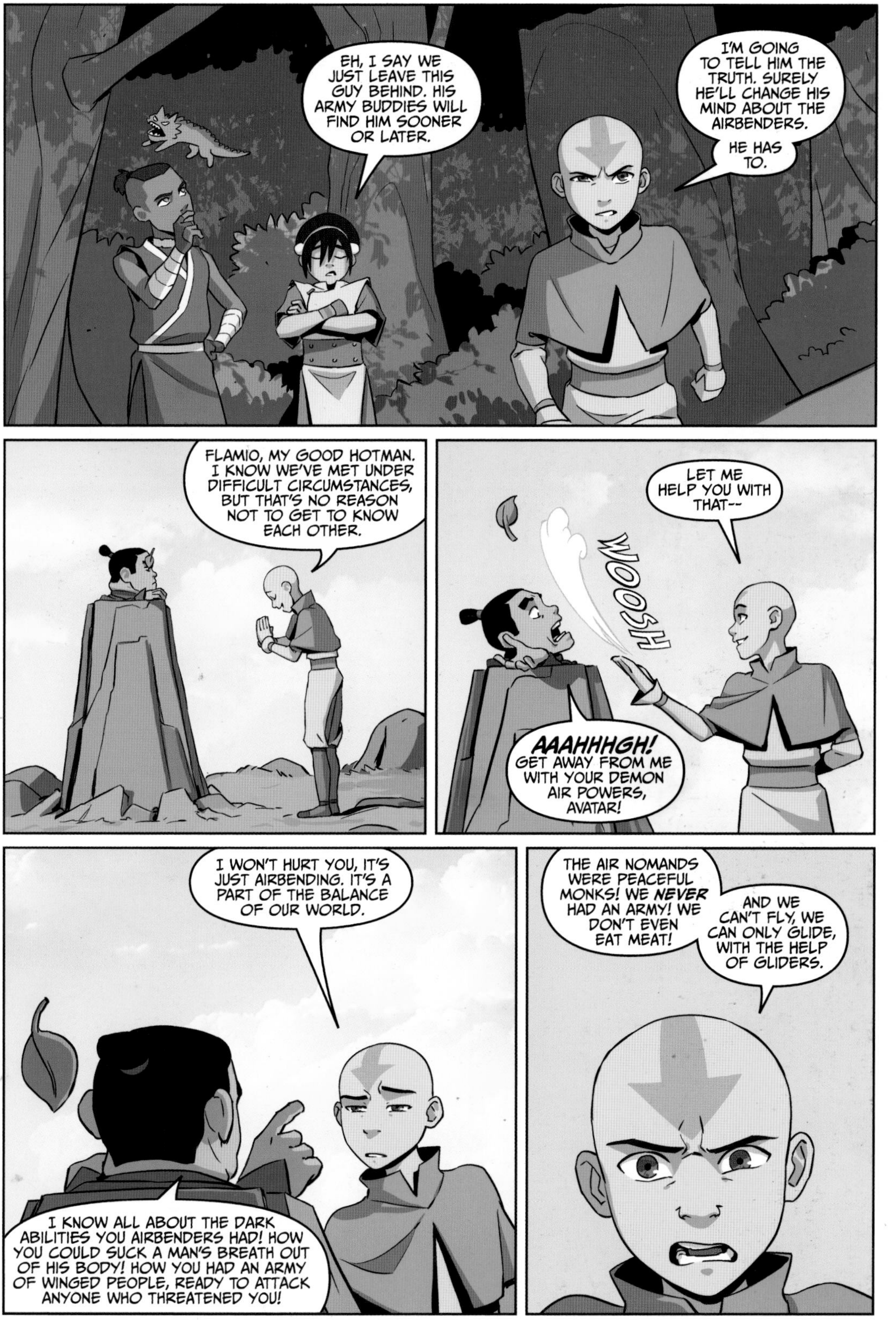
EH, I SAY WE JUST LEAVE THIS GUY BEHIND. HIS ARMY BUDDIES WILL FIND HIM SOONER OR LATER.
I'M GOING TO TELL HIM THE TRUTH. SURELY HE'LL CHANGE HIS MIND ABOUT THE AIRBENDERS.
HE HAS TO.
FLAMIO, MY GOOD HOTMAN. I KNOW WE'VE MET UNDER DIFFICULT CIRCUMSTANCES, BUT THAT'S NO REASON NOT TO GET TO KNOW EACH OTHER.
LET ME HELP YOU WITH THAT--
WOOSH
AAAHHHGH! GET AWAY FROM ME WITH YOUR DEMON AIR POWERS, AVATAR!
I WON'T HURT YOU, IT'S JUST AIRBENDING. IT'S A PART OF THE BALANCE OF OUR WORLD.
I KNOW ALL ABOUT THE DARK ABILITIES YOU AIRBENDERS HAD! HOW YOU COULD SUCK A MAN'S BREATH OUT OF HIS BODY! HOW YOU HAD AN ARMY OF WINGED PEOPLE, READY TO ATTACK ANYONE WHO THREATENED YOU!
THE AIR NOMANDS WERE PEACEFUL MONKS! WE NEVER HAD AN ARMY! WE DON'T EVEN EAT MEAT!
AND WE CAN'T FLY, WE CAN ONLY GLIDE, WITH THE HELP OF GLIDERS.

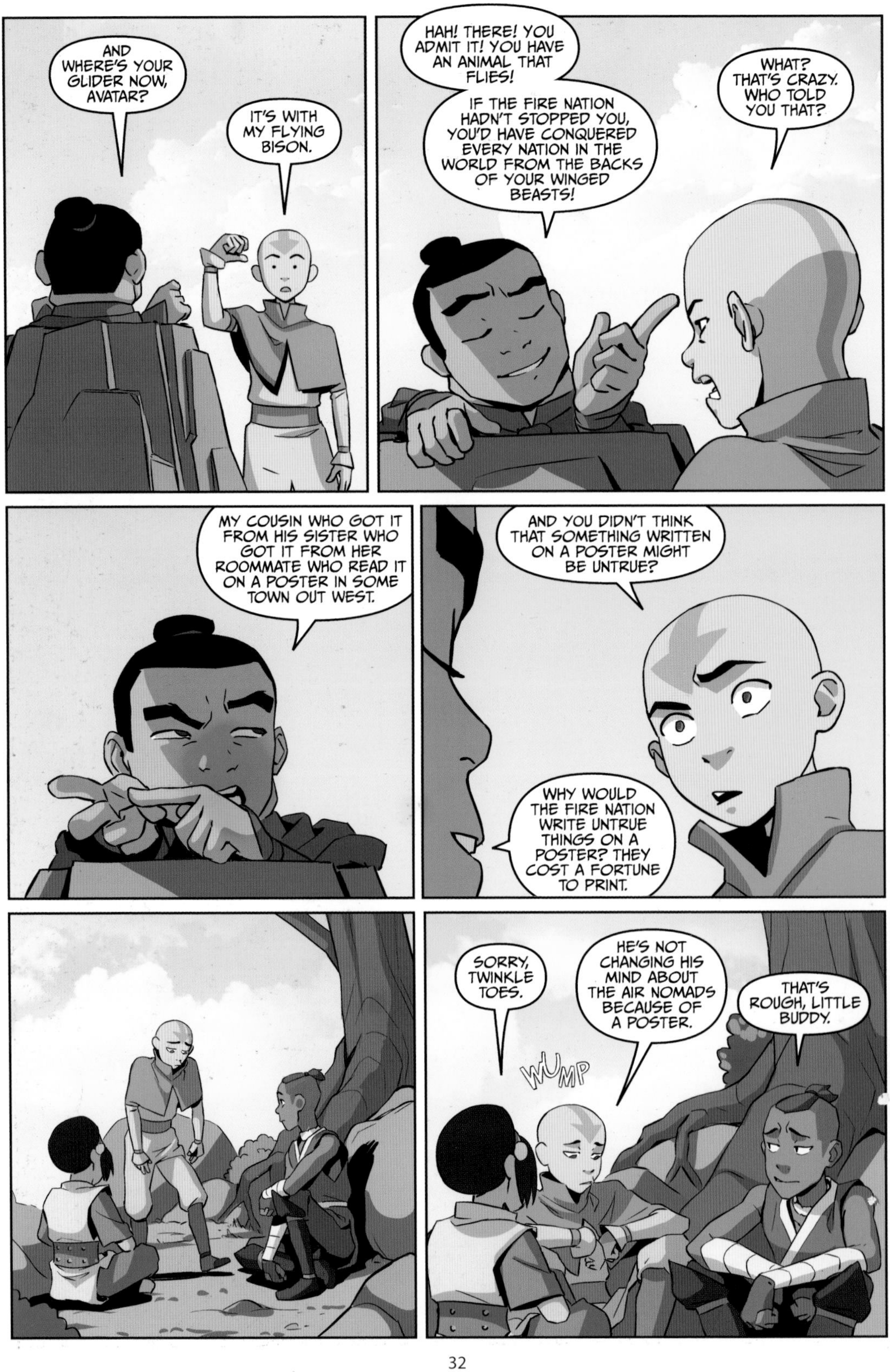
AND WHERE'S YOUR GLIDER NOW, AVATAR?
IT'S WITH MY FLYING BISON.
HAH! THERE! YOU ADMIT IT! YOU HAVE AN ANIMAL THAT FLIES!
IF THE FIRE NATION HADN'T STOPPED YOU, YOU'D HAVE CONQUERED EVERY NATION IN THE WORLD FROM THE BACKS OF YOUR WINGED BEASTS!
WHAT? THAT'S CRAZY. WHO TOLD YOU THAT?
MY COUSIN WHO GOT IT FROM HIS SISTER WHO GOT IT FROM HER ROOMMATE WHO READ IT ON A POSTER IN SOME TOWN OUT WEST.
AND YOU DIDN'T THINK THAT SOMETHING WRITTEN ON A POSTER MIGHT BE UNTRUE?
WHY WOULD THE FIRE NATION WRITE UNTRUE THINGS ON A POSTER? THEY COST A FORTUNE TO PRINT.
SORRY, TWINKLE TOES.
HE'S NOT CHANGING HIS MIND ABOUT THE AIR NOMADS BECAUSE OF A POSTER.
WUMP
THAT'S ROUGH, LITTLE BUDDY.

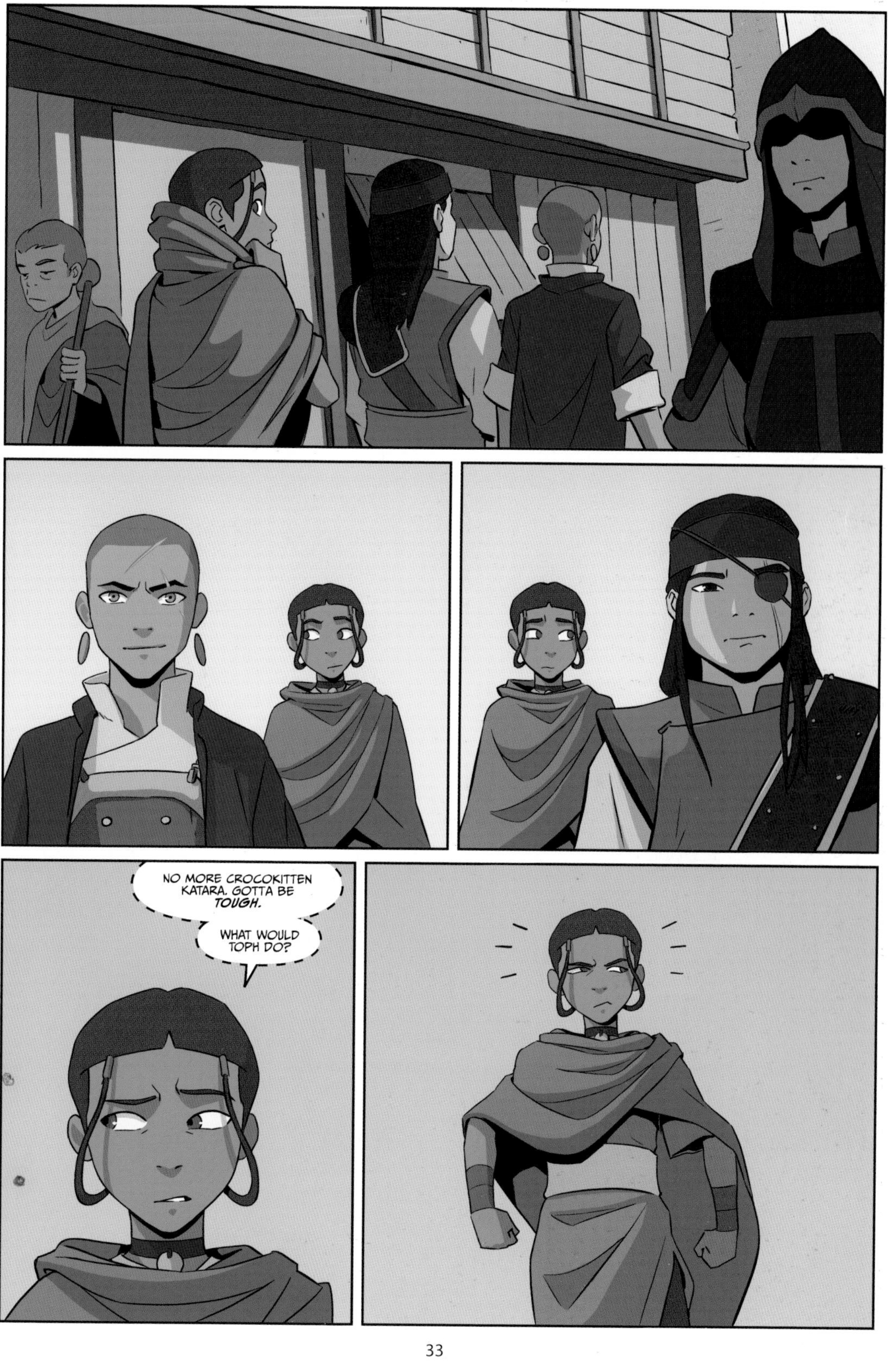
NO MORE CROCOKITTEN KATARA. GOTTA BE TOUGH.
WHAT WOULD TOPH DO?

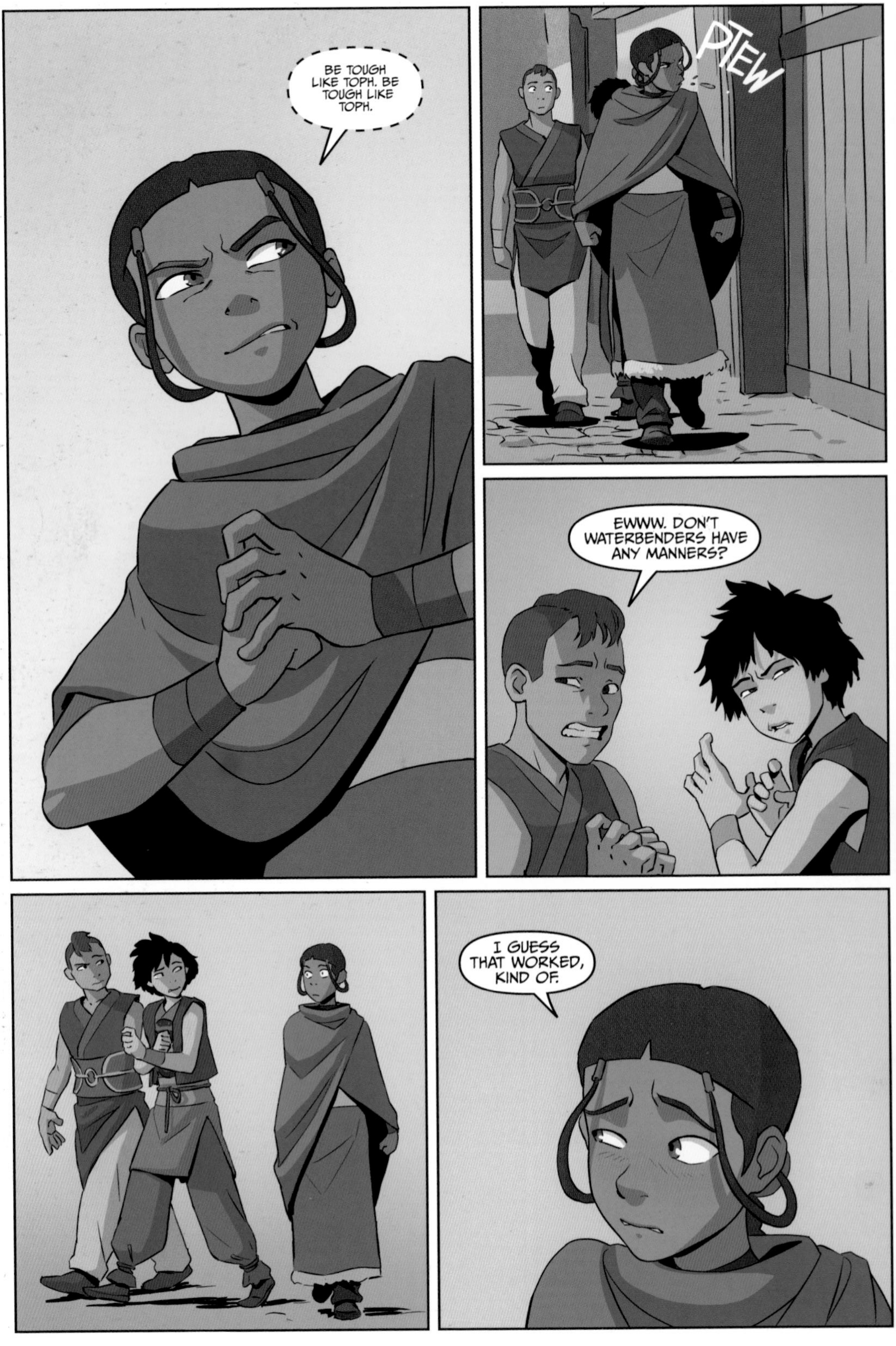
BE TOUGH LIKE TOPH. BE TOUGH LIKE TOPH.
PTEW
EWWW. DON'T WATERBENDERS HAVE ANY MANNERS?
I GUESS THAT WORKED, KIND OF.

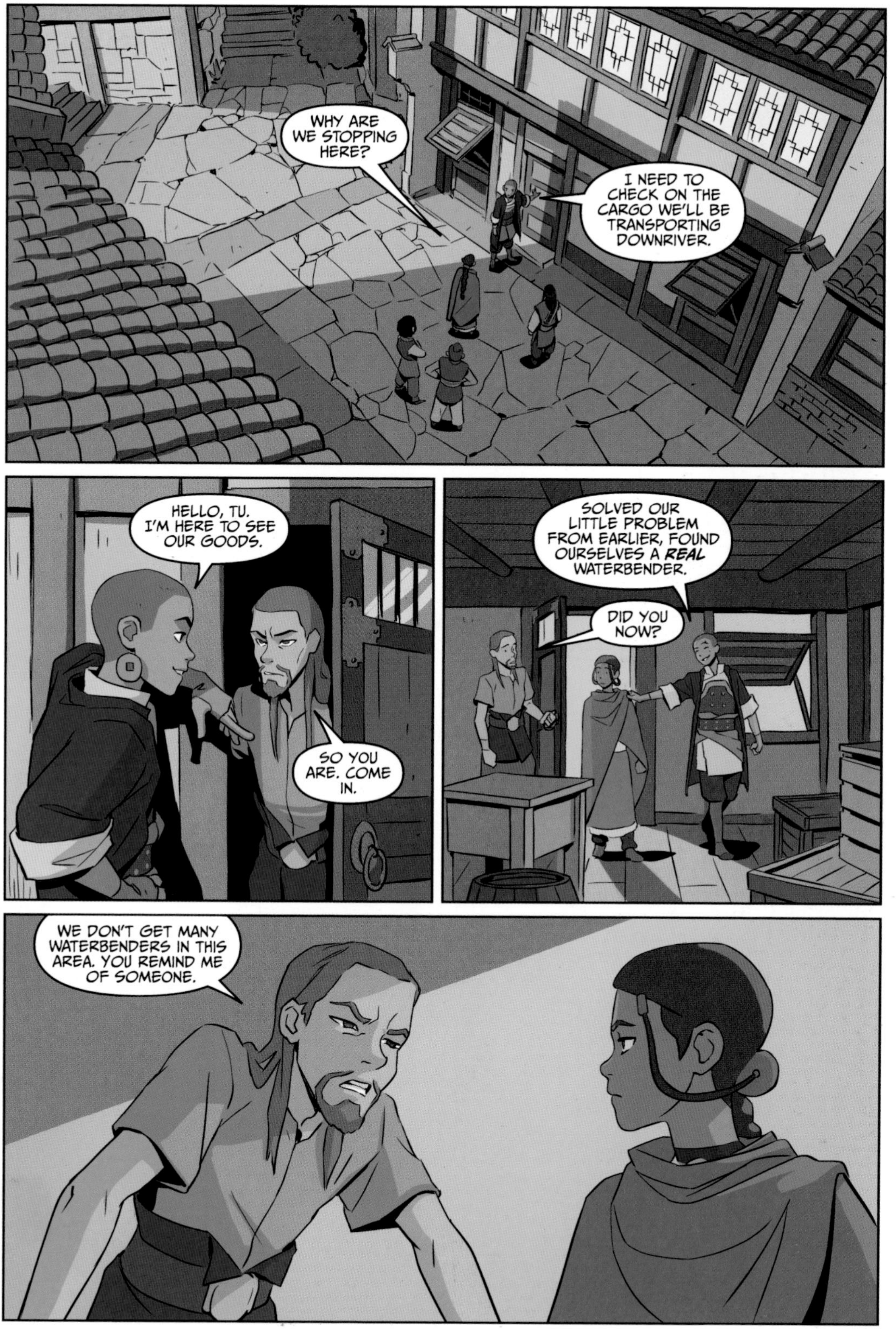
WHY ARE WE STOPPING HERE?
I NEED TO CHECK ON THE CARGO WE'LL BE TRANSPORTING DOWNRIVER.
HELLO, TU. I'M HERE TO SEE OUR GOODS.
SO YOU ARE. COME IN.
SOLVED OUR LITTLE PROBLEM FROM EARLIER, FOUND OURSELVES A *REAL* WATERBENDER.
DID YOU NOW?
WE DON'T GET MANY WATERBENDERS IN THIS AREA. YOU REMIND ME OF SOMEONE.

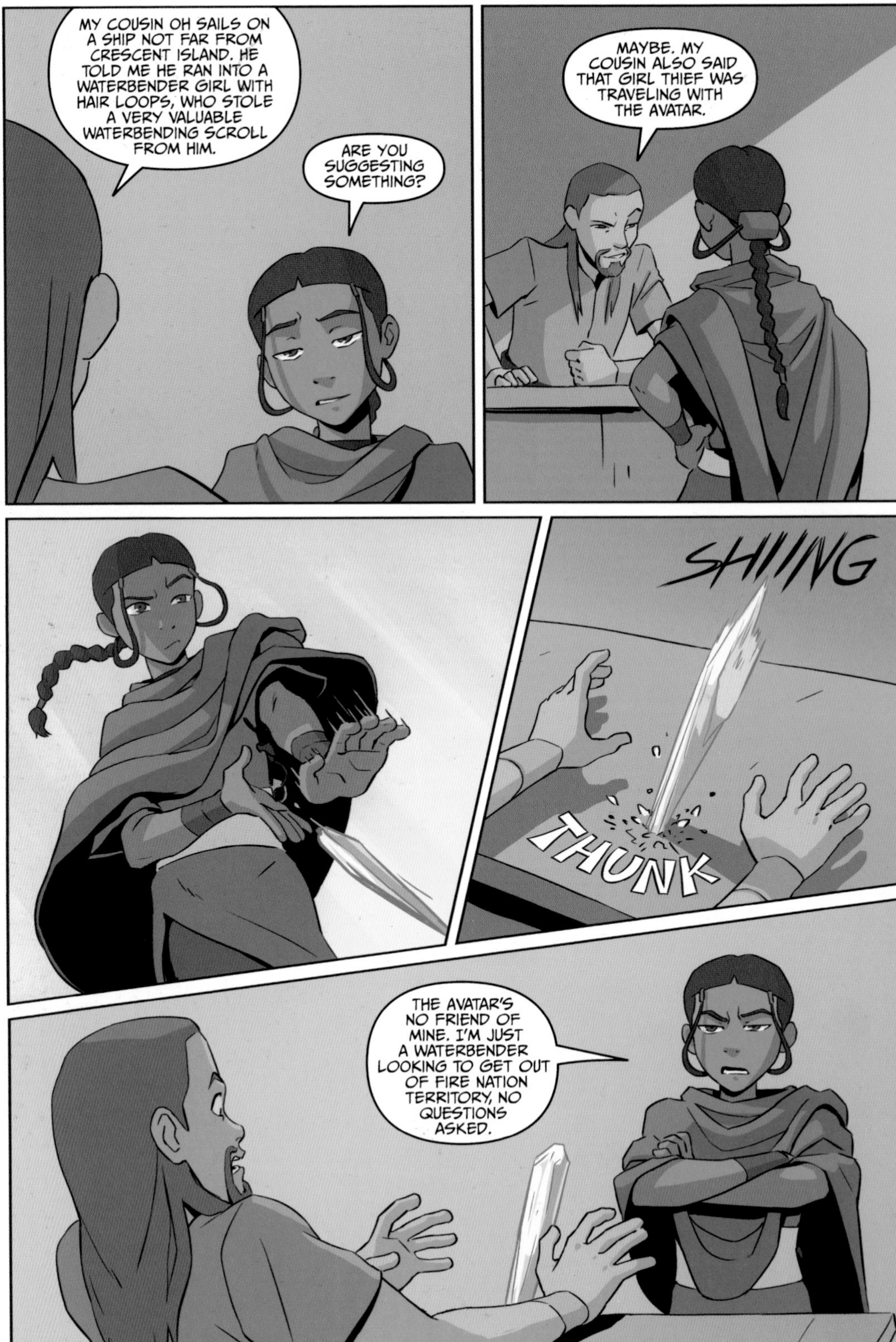

MY COUSIN OH SAILS ON A SHIP NOT FAR FROM CRESCENT ISLAND. HE TOLD ME HE RAN INTO A WATERBENDER GIRL WITH HAIR LOOPS, WHO STOLE A VERY VALUABLE WATERBENDING SCROLL FROM HIM.
ARE YOU SUGGESTING SOMETHING?
MAYBE. MY COUSIN ALSO SAID THAT GIRL THIEF WAS TRAVELING WITH THE AVATAR.
SHIING
THUNK
THE AVATAR'S NO FRIEND OF MINE. I'M JUST A WATERBENDER LOOKING TO GET OUT OF FIRE NATION TERRITORY, NO QUESTIONS ASKED.

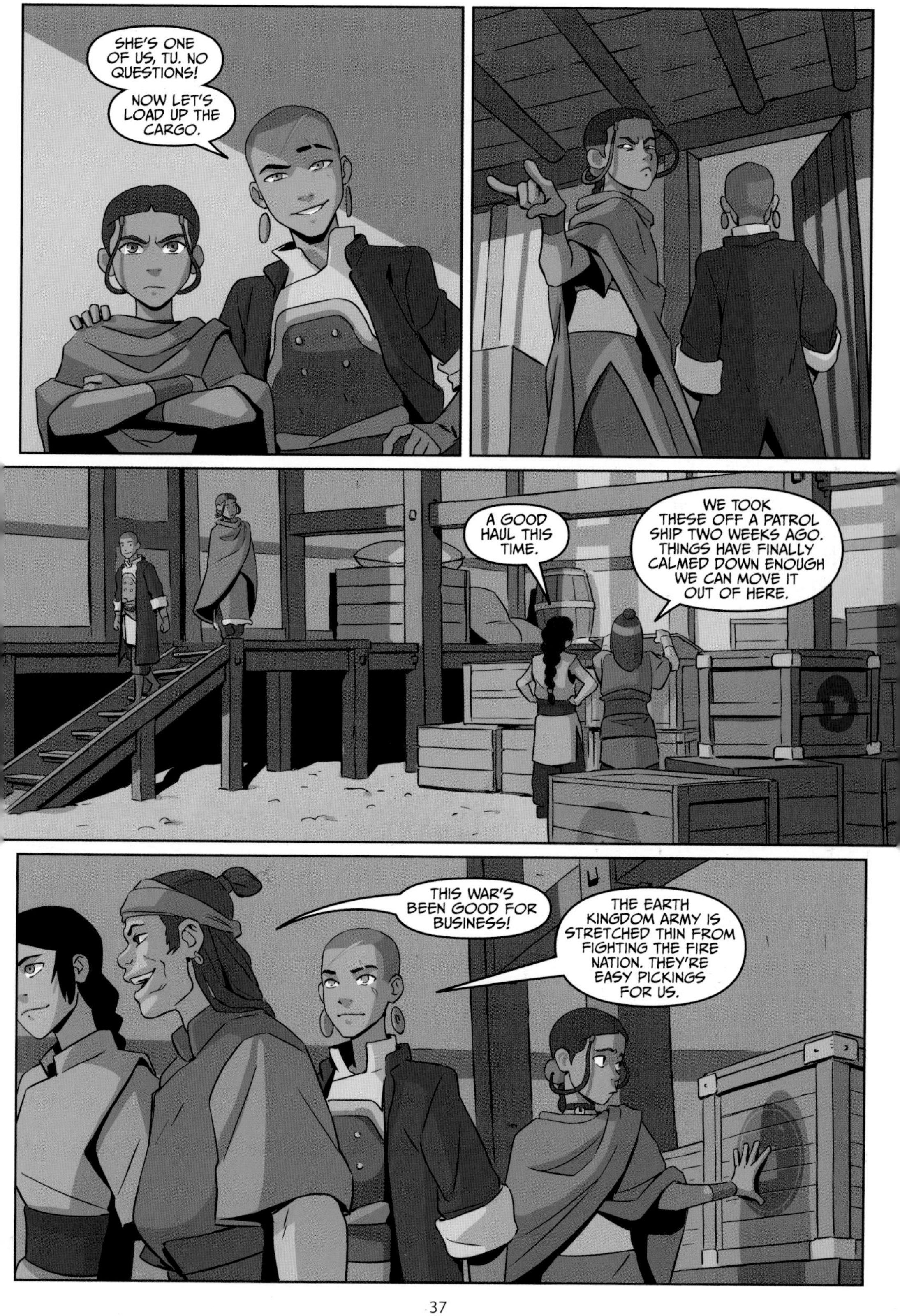
SHE'S ONE OF US, TU. NO QUESTIONS!
NOW LET'S LOAD UP THE CARGO.
A GOOD HAUL THIS TIME.
WE TOOK THESE OFF A PATROL SHIP TWO WEEKS AGO. THINGS HAVE FINALLY CALMED DOWN ENOUGH WE CAN MOVE IT OUT OF HERE.
THIS WAR'S BEEN GOOD FOR BUSINESS!
THE EARTH KINGDOM ARMY IS STRETCHED THIN FROM FIGHTING THE FIRE NATION. THEY'RE EASY PICKINGS FOR US.

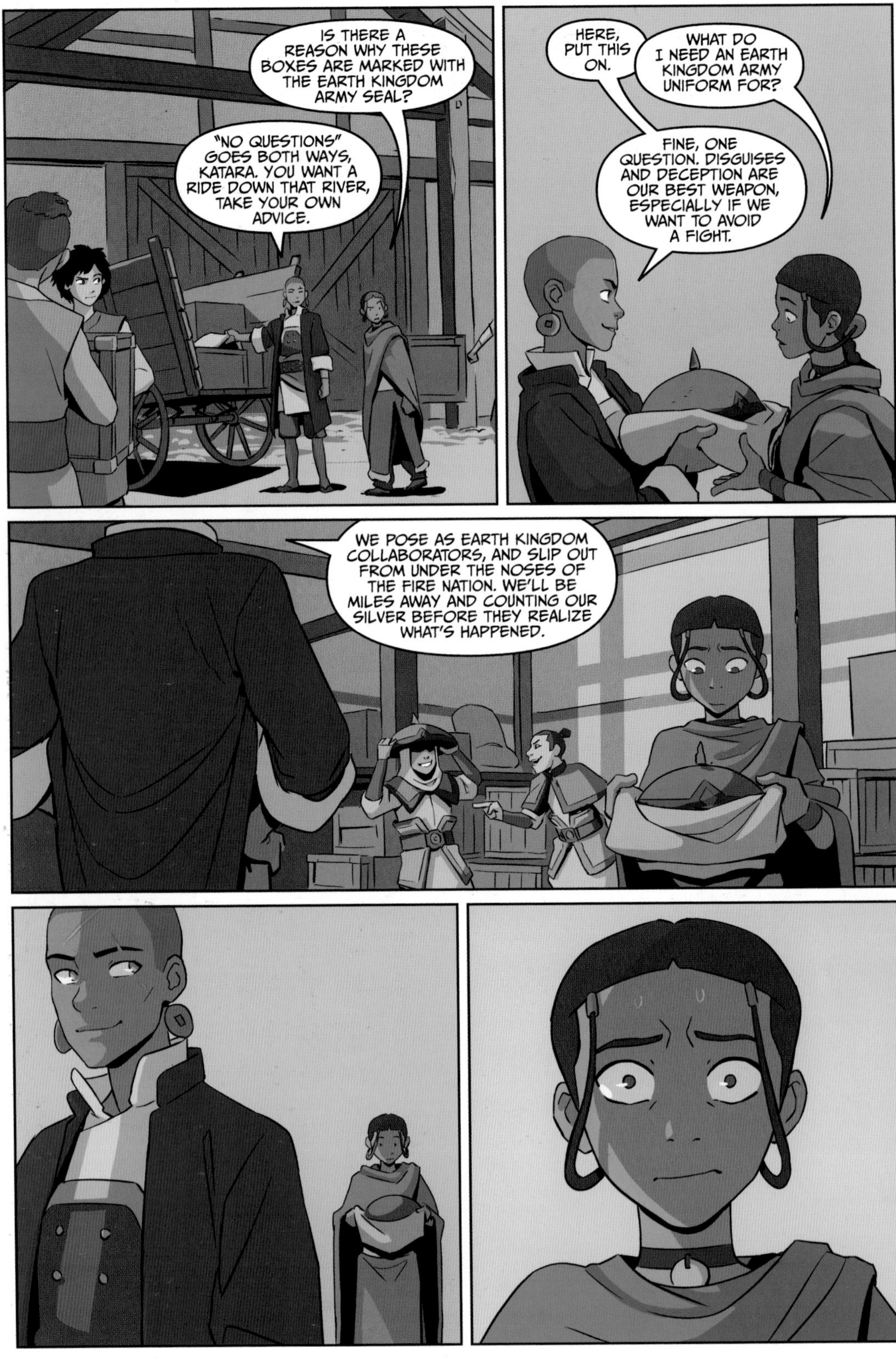
IS THERE A REASON WHY THESE BOXES ARE MARKED WITH THE EARTH KINGDOM ARMY SEAL?
"NO QUESTIONS" GOES BOTH WAYS, KATARA. YOU WANT A RIDE DOWN THAT RIVER, TAKE YOUR OWN ADVICE.
HERE, PUT THIS ON.
WHAT DO I NEED AN EARTH KINGDOM ARMY UNIFORM FOR?
FINE, ONE QUESTION. DISGUISES AND DECEPTION ARE OUR BEST WEAPON, ESPECIALLY IF WE WANT TO AVOID A FIGHT.
WE POSE AS EARTH KINGDOM COLLABORATORS, AND SLIP OUT FROM UNDER THE NOSES OF THE FIRE NATION. WE'LL BE MILES AWAY AND COUNTING OUR SILVER BEFORE THEY REALIZE WHAT'S HAPPENED.

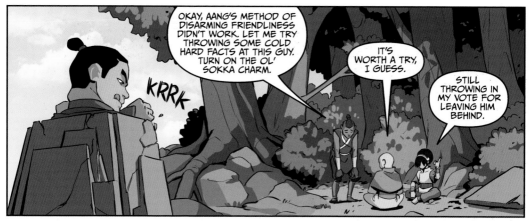

OKAY, AANG'S METHOD OF DISARMING FRIENDLINESS DIDN'T WORK. LET ME TRY THROWING SOME COLD HARD FACTS AT THIS GUY. TURN ON THE OL' SOKKA CHARM.

KRRK

IT'S WORTH A TRY, I GUESS.

STILL THROWING IN MY VOTE FOR LEAVING HIM BEHIND.

MY GOOD HOTMAN, EVEN IF YOU DON'T BELIEVE WHAT AANG TOLD YOU ABOUT THE AIR NOMADS, WE DON'T HAVE TO BE ENEMIES.

AS LONG AS YOU *STAND AGAINST* THE FIRE LORD, YOU ARE MY ENEMY.

KRRK

THAT'S THE THING, WE DON'T *WANT* TO BE THE FIRE LORD'S ENEMY. WE'D ACTUALLY *LOVE* TO LIVE IN HARMONY WITH HIM AND THE REST OF THE FIRE NATION.

WHAT?

FOR EXAMPLE, ISN'T IT A BIT *ODD* THAT YOU'RE FIRE NATION, BUT YOU'VE BEEN SENT TO THE EARTH KINGDOM TO OCCUPY IT?

OF COURSE NOT! THE FIRE NATION IS SHARING ITS WEALTH AND ACHIEVEMENTS WITH THE REST OF THE WORLD. THE OTHER NATIONS SHOULD BE *HONORED* THAT WE'RE HERE!

THINK ABOUT THAT FOR A MOMENT. DO EARTH KINGDOM CITIZENS WELCOME YOU INTO THEIR HOMES? DID THEY OPEN THE GATES OF BA SING SE TO THE FIRE NATION ARMIES?

WELL, NO. NOT AT FIRST.

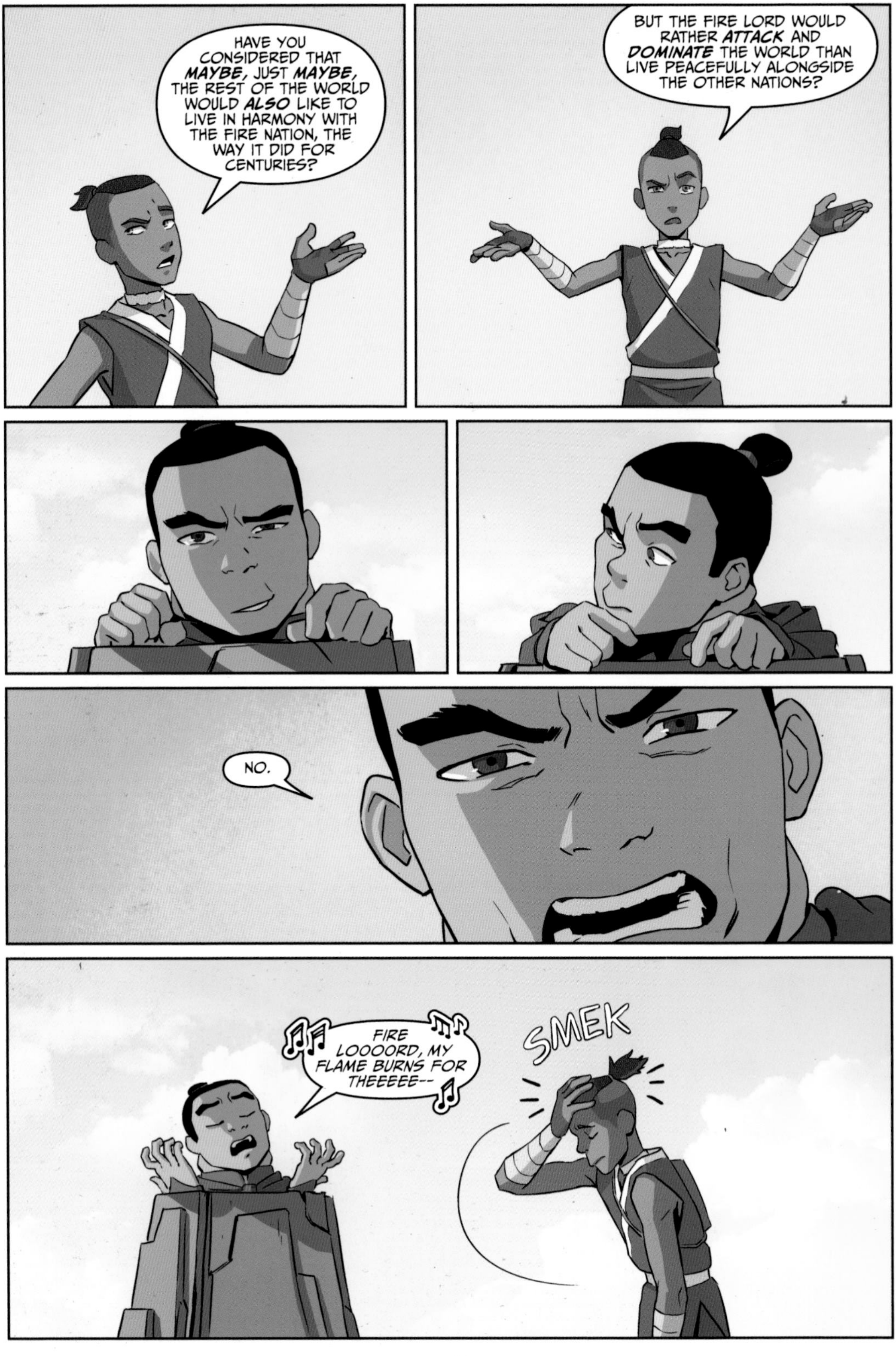
HAVE YOU CONSIDERED THAT MAYBE, JUST MAYBE, THE REST OF THE WORLD WOULD ALSO LIKE TO LIVE IN HARMONY WITH THE FIRE NATION, THE WAY IT DID FOR CENTURIES?
BUT THE FIRE LORD WOULD RATHER ATTACK AND DOMINATE THE WORLD THAN LIVE PEACEFULLY ALONGSIDE THE OTHER NATIONS?
NO.
FIRE LOOOORD, MY FLAME BURNS FOR THEEEEE--
SMEK

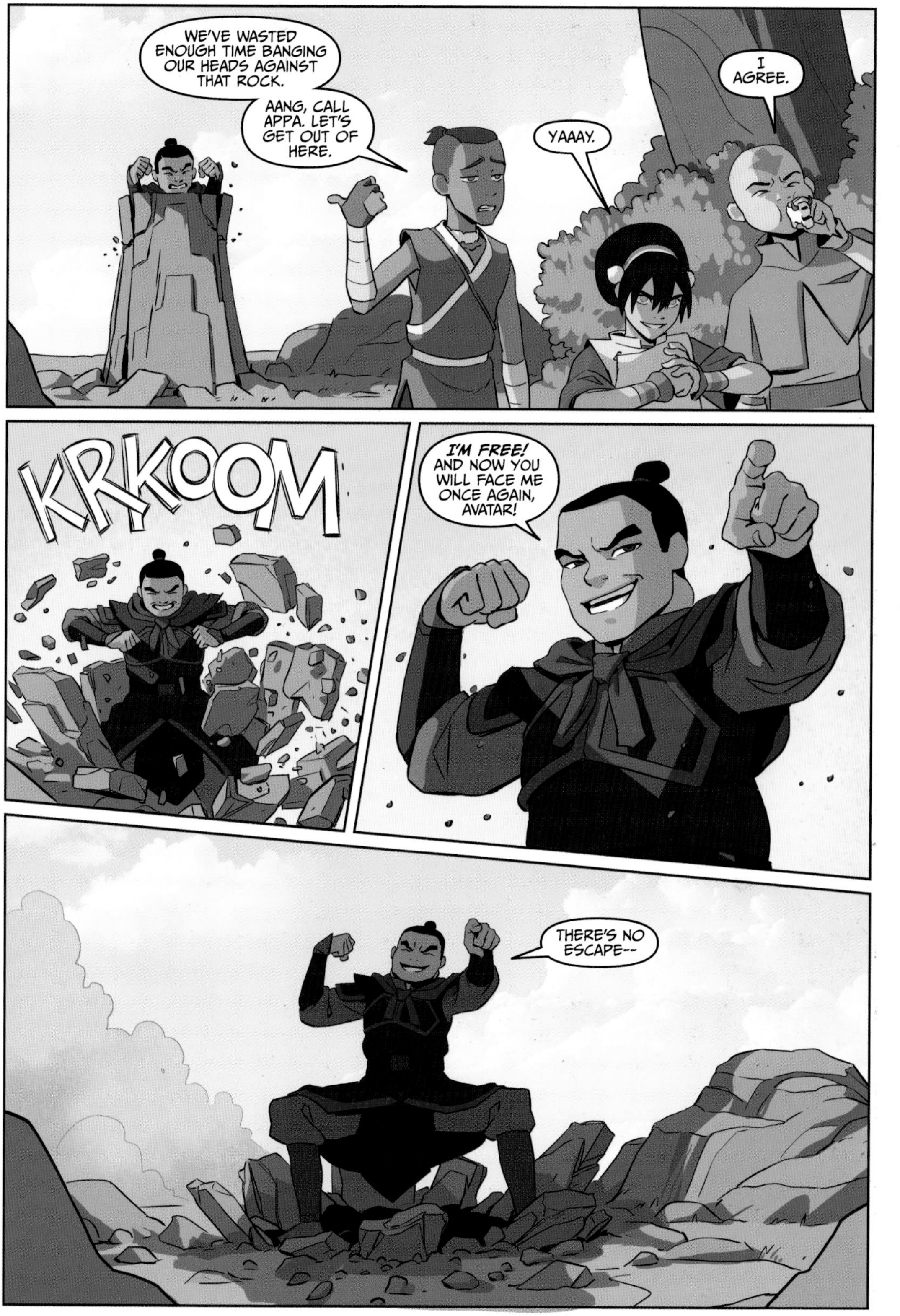
WE'VE WASTED ENOUGH TIME BANGING OUR HEADS AGAINST THAT ROCK.
AANG, CALL APPA. LET'S GET OUT OF HERE.
YAAAY.
I AGREE.
KRKOOM
I'M FREE! AND NOW YOU WILL FACE ME ONCE AGAIN, AVATAR!
THERE'S NO ESCAPE--

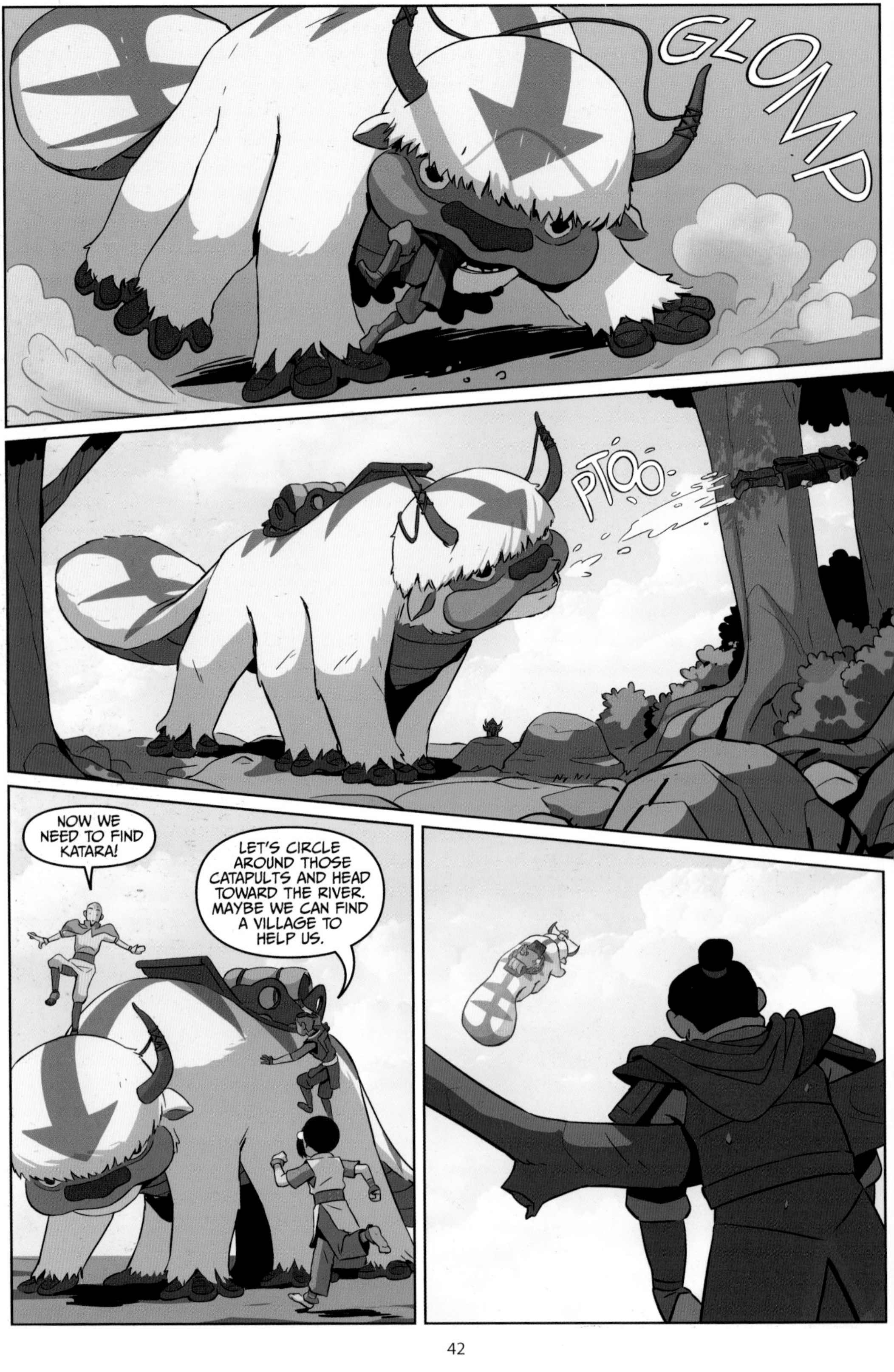
GLOMP
PTOO
NOW WE NEED TO FIND KATARA!
LET'S CIRCLE AROUND THOSE CATAPULTS AND HEAD TOWARD THE RIVER. MAYBE WE CAN FIND A VILLAGE TO HELP US.

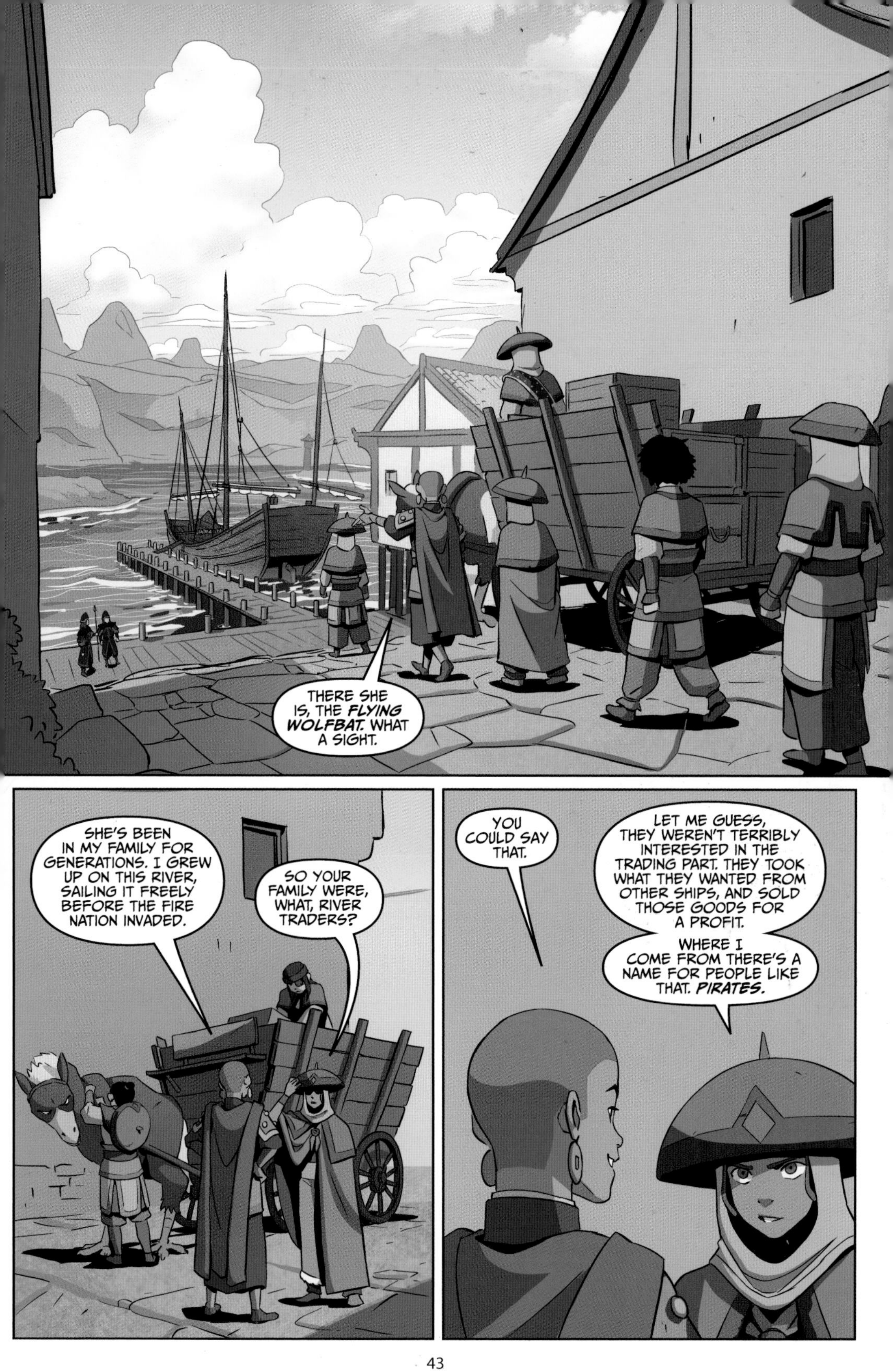
THERE SHE IS, THE ***FLYING WOLFBAT.*** WHAT A SIGHT.
SHE'S BEEN IN MY FAMILY FOR GENERATIONS. I GREW UP ON THIS RIVER, SAILING IT FREELY BEFORE THE FIRE NATION INVADED.
SO YOUR FAMILY WERE, WHAT, RIVER TRADERS?
YOU COULD SAY THAT.
LET ME GUESS, THEY WEREN'T TERRIBLY INTERESTED IN THE TRADING PART. THEY TOOK WHAT THEY WANTED FROM OTHER SHIPS, AND SOLD THOSE GOODS FOR A PROFIT.
WHERE I COME FROM THERE'S A NAME FOR PEOPLE LIKE THAT. ***PIRATES.***

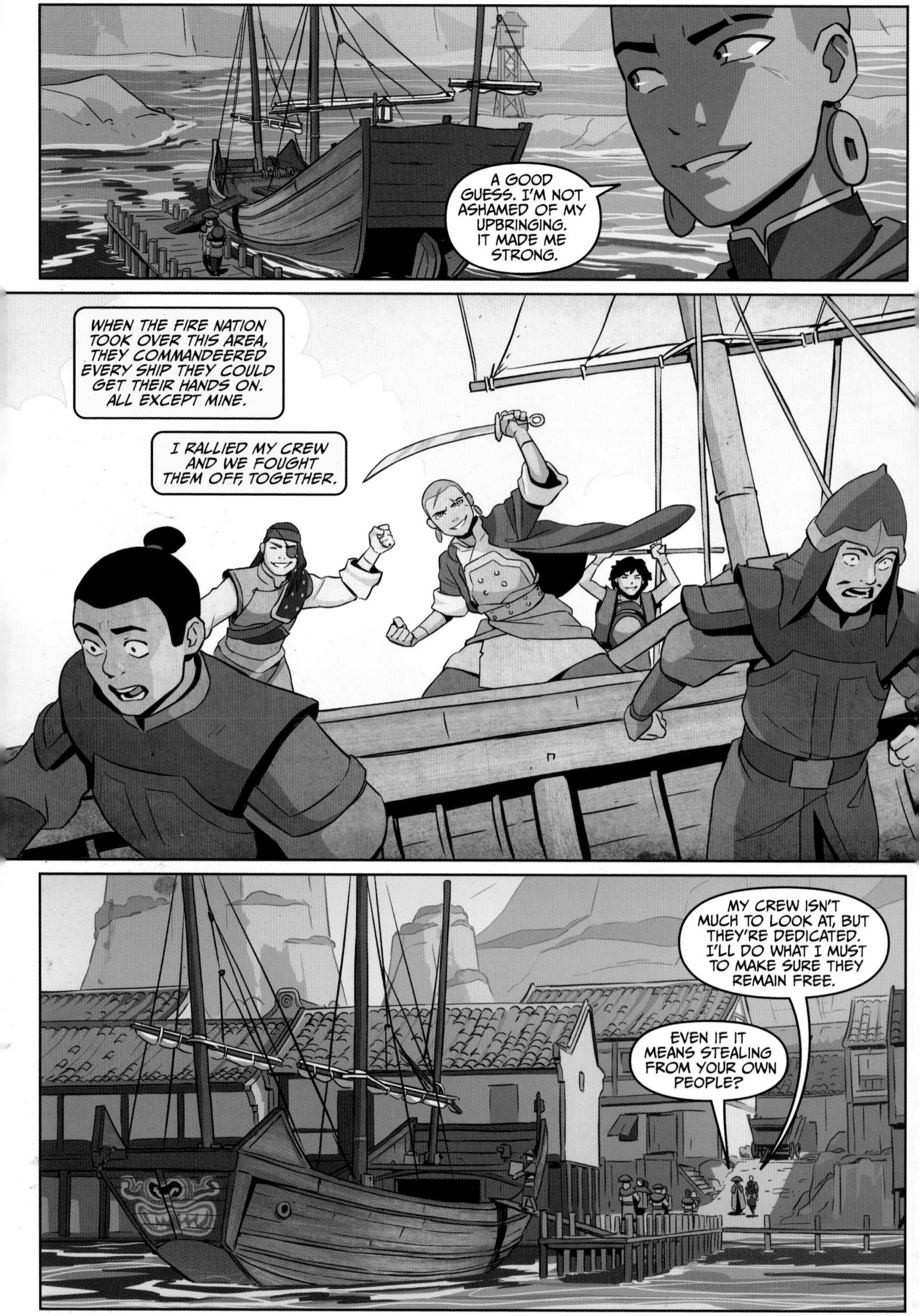
A GOOD GUESS. I'M NOT ASHAMED OF MY UPBRINGING. IT MADE ME STRONG.
WHEN THE FIRE NATION TOOK OVER THIS AREA, THEY COMMANDEERED EVERY SHIP THEY COULD GET THEIR HANDS ON. ALL EXCEPT MINE.
I RALLIED MY CREW AND WE FOUGHT THEM OFF, TOGETHER.
MY CREW ISN'T MUCH TO LOOK AT, BUT THEY'RE DEDICATED. I'LL DO WHAT I MUST TO MAKE SURE THEY REMAIN FREE.
EVEN IF IT MEANS STEALING FROM YOUR OWN PEOPLE?

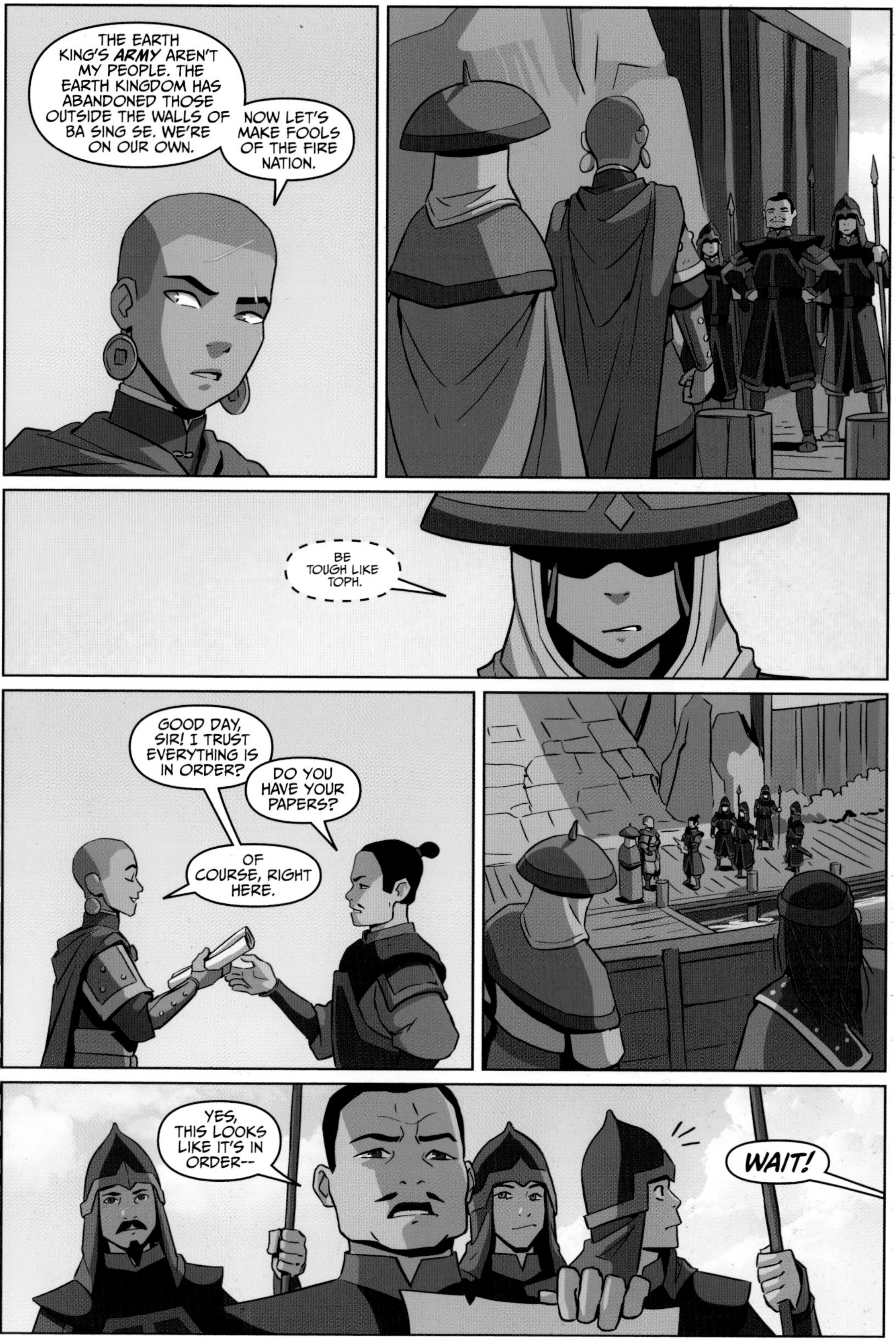
THE EARTH KING'S ARMY AREN'T MY PEOPLE. THE EARTH KINGDOM HAS ABANDONED THOSE OUTSIDE THE WALLS OF BA SING SE. WE'RE ON OUR OWN.
NOW LET'S MAKE FOOLS OF THE FIRE NATION.
BE TOUGH LIKE TOPH.
GOOD DAY, SIR! I TRUST EVERYTHING IS IN ORDER?
DO YOU HAVE YOUR PAPERS?
OF COURSE, RIGHT HERE.
YES, THIS LOOKS LIKE IT'S IN ORDER--
WAIT!

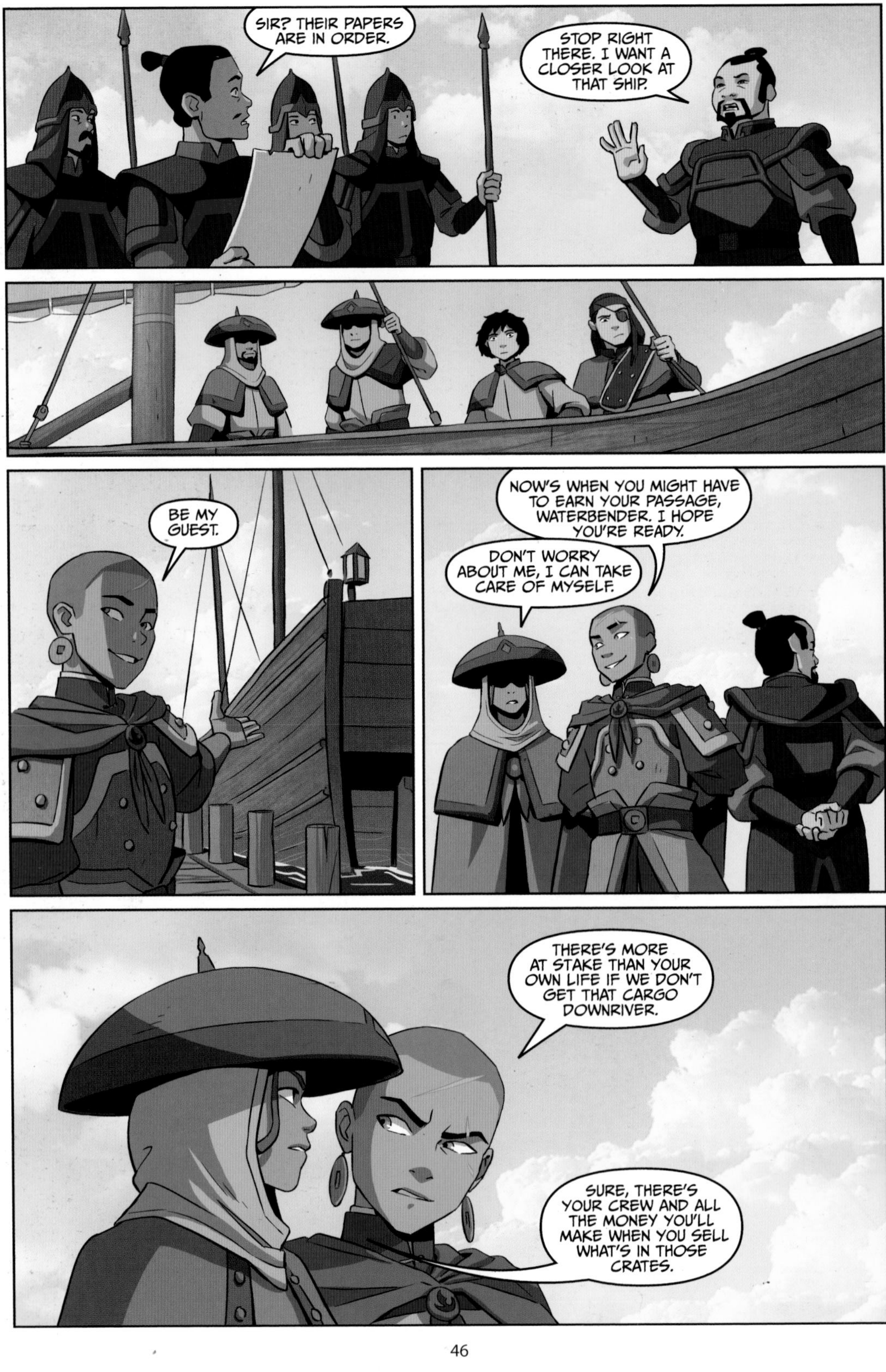
SIR? THEIR PAPERS ARE IN ORDER.
STOP RIGHT THERE. I WANT A CLOSER LOOK AT THAT SHIP.
BE MY GUEST.
NOW'S WHEN YOU MIGHT HAVE TO EARN YOUR PASSAGE, WATERBENDER. I HOPE YOU'RE READY.
DON'T WORRY ABOUT ME, I CAN TAKE CARE OF MYSELF.
THERE'S MORE AT STAKE THAN YOUR OWN LIFE IF WE DON'T GET THAT CARGO DOWNRIVER.
SURE, THERE'S YOUR CREW AND ALL THE MONEY YOU'LL MAKE WHEN YOU SELL WHAT'S IN THOSE CRATES.

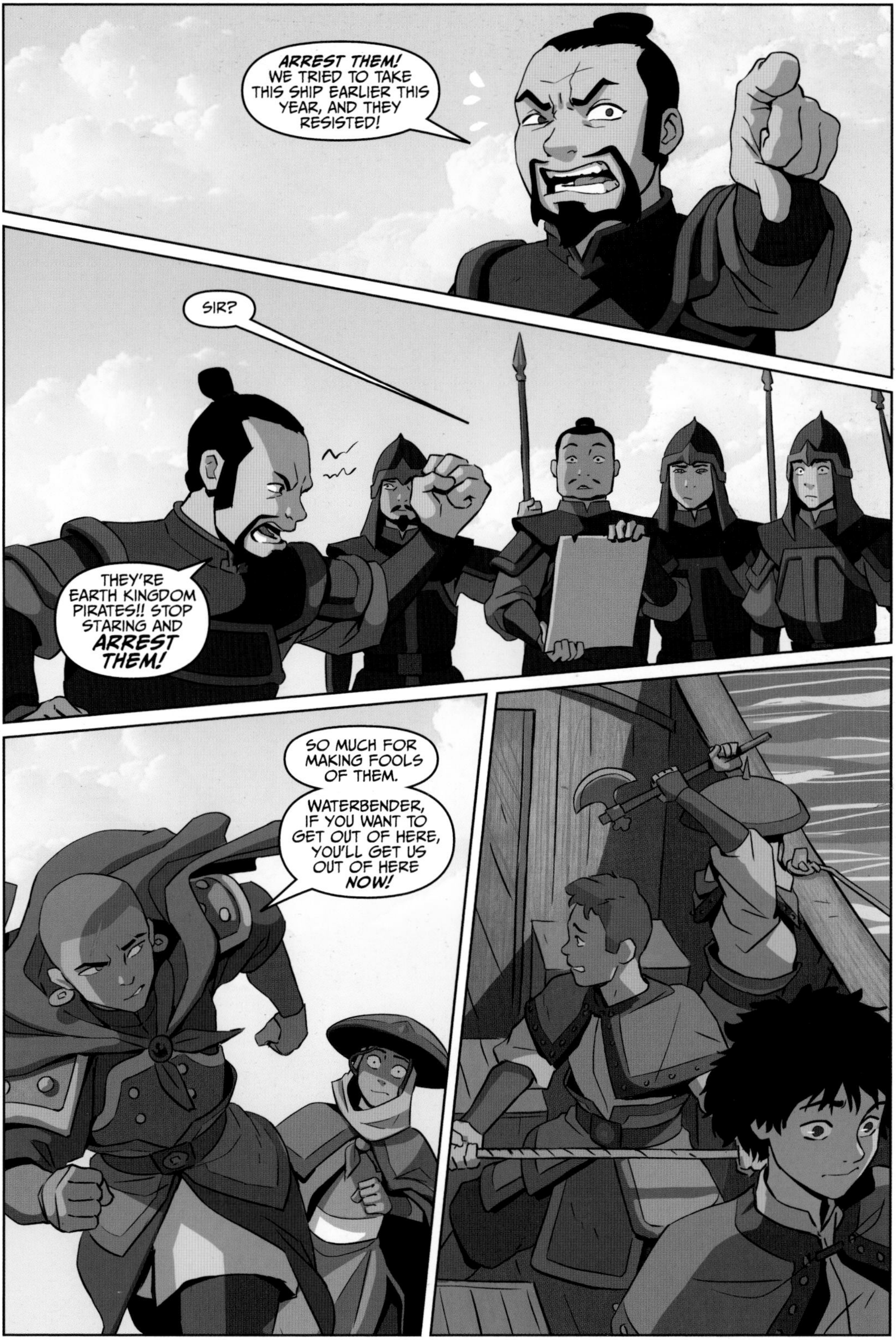
ARREST THEM! WE TRIED TO TAKE THIS SHIP EARLIER THIS YEAR, AND THEY RESISTED!
SIR?
THEY'RE EARTH KINGDOM PIRATES!! STOP STARING AND ARREST THEM!
SO MUCH FOR MAKING FOOLS OF THEM.
WATERBENDER, IF YOU WANT TO GET OUT OF HERE, YOU'LL GET US OUT OF HERE NOW!

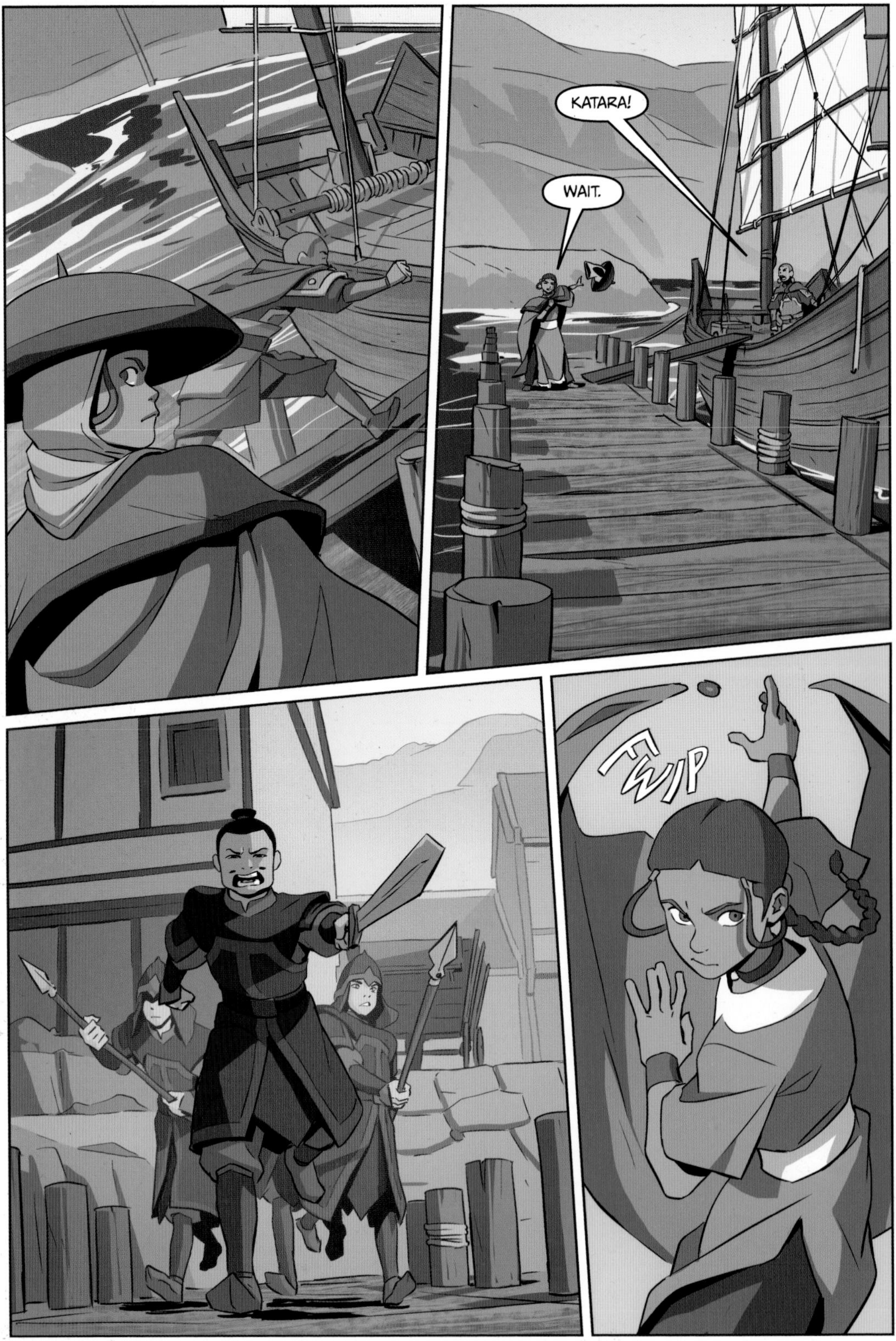
KATARA!
WAIT.
FWIP

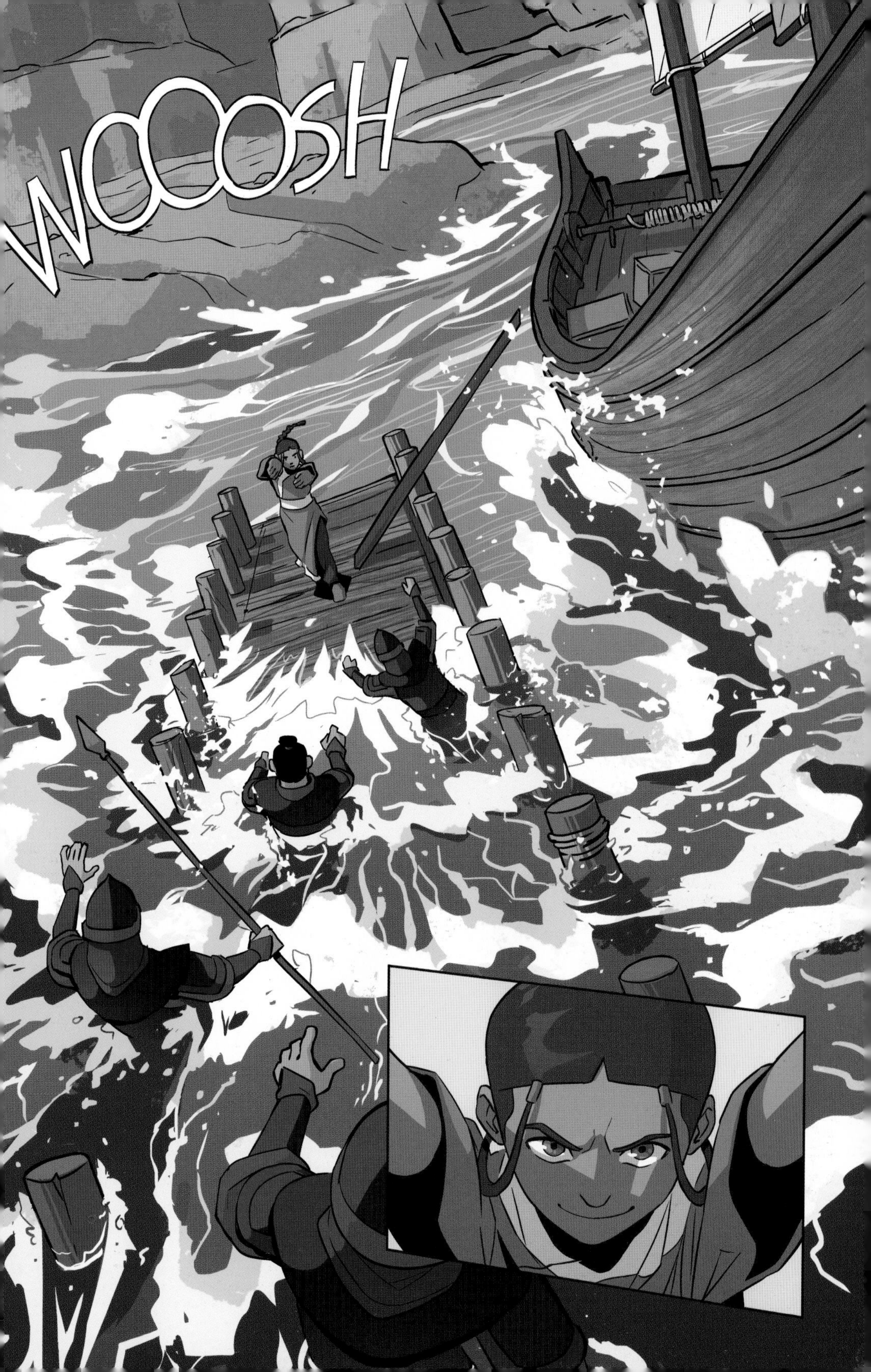
WOOOSH

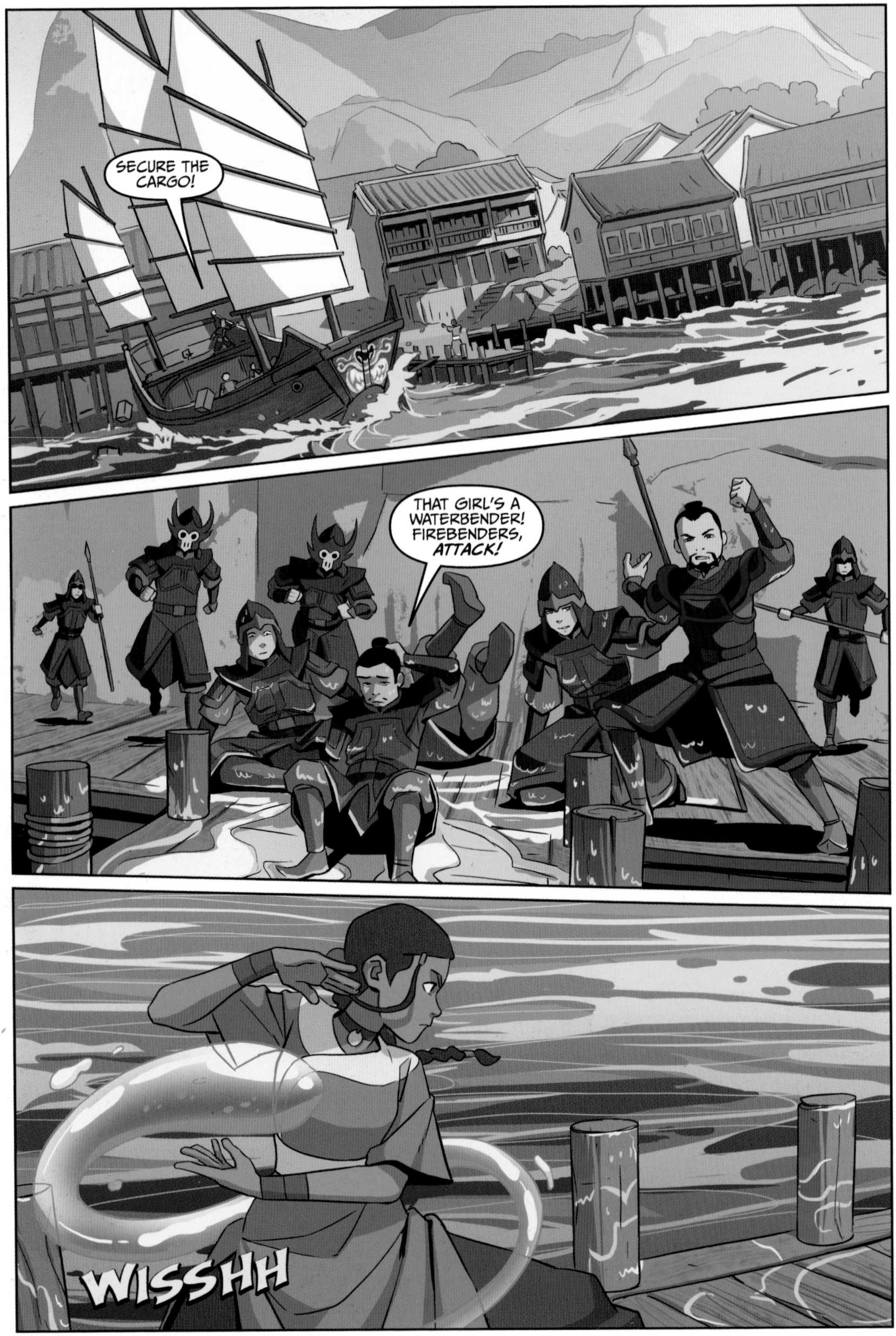
SECURE THE CARGO!
THAT GIRL'S A WATERBENDER! FIREBENDERS, ATTACK!
WISSHH

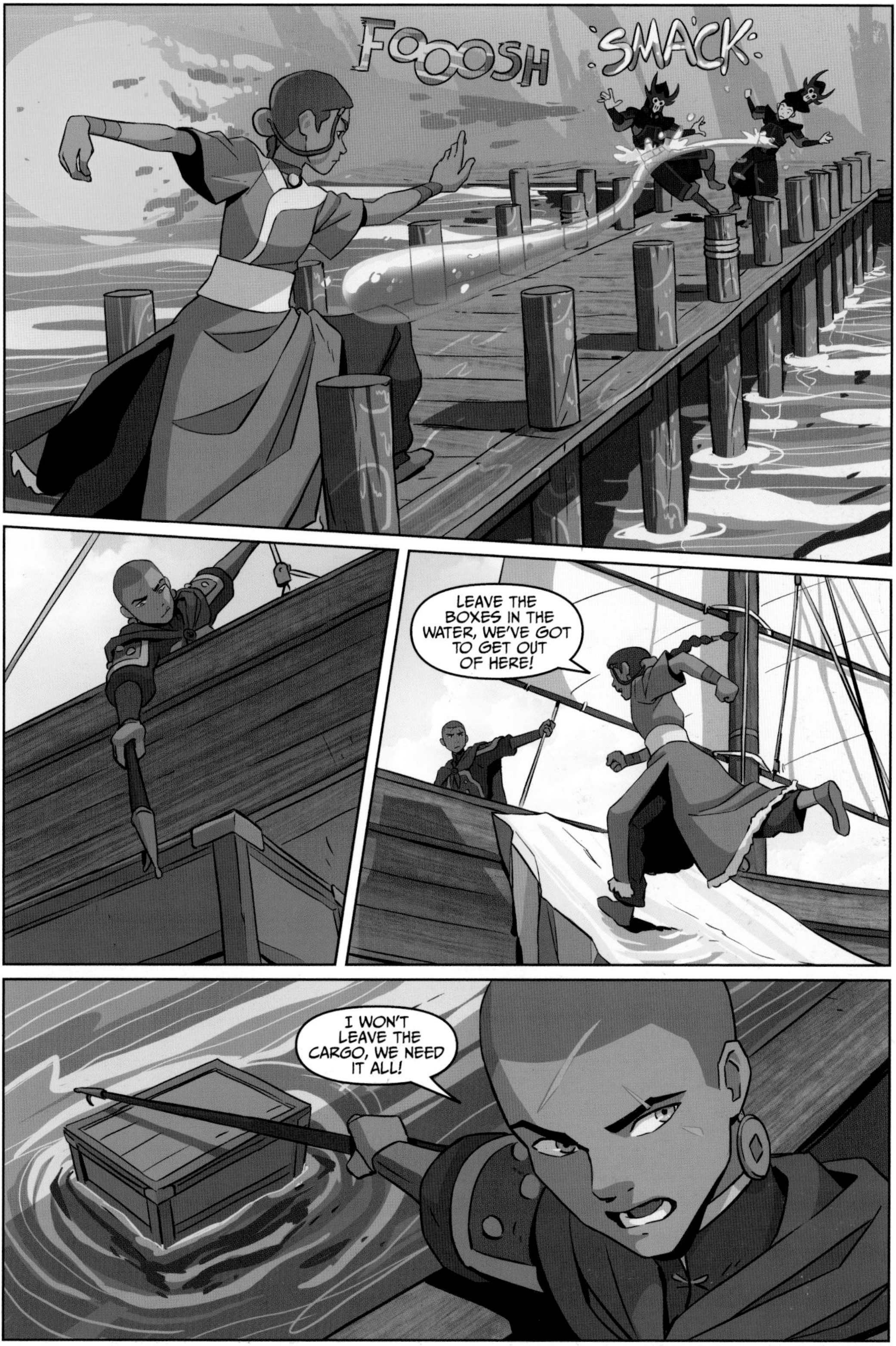
FOOOSH
SMACK
LEAVE THE BOXES IN THE WATER, WE'VE GOT TO GET OUT OF HERE!
I WON'T LEAVE THE CARGO, WE NEED IT ALL!

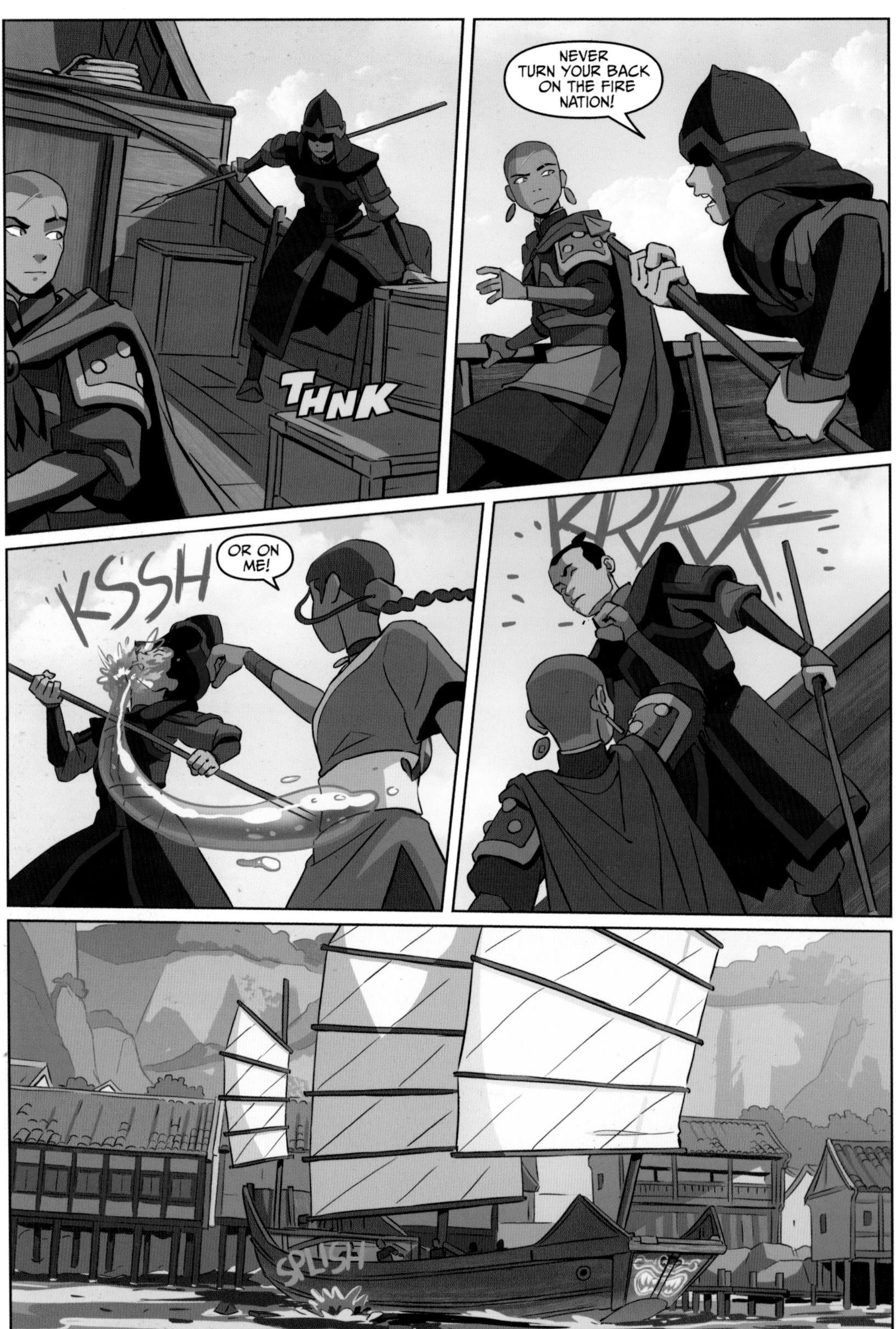
THNK
NEVER TURN YOUR BACK ON THE FIRE NATION!
KSSH
OR ON ME!
KRRRK
SPLISH

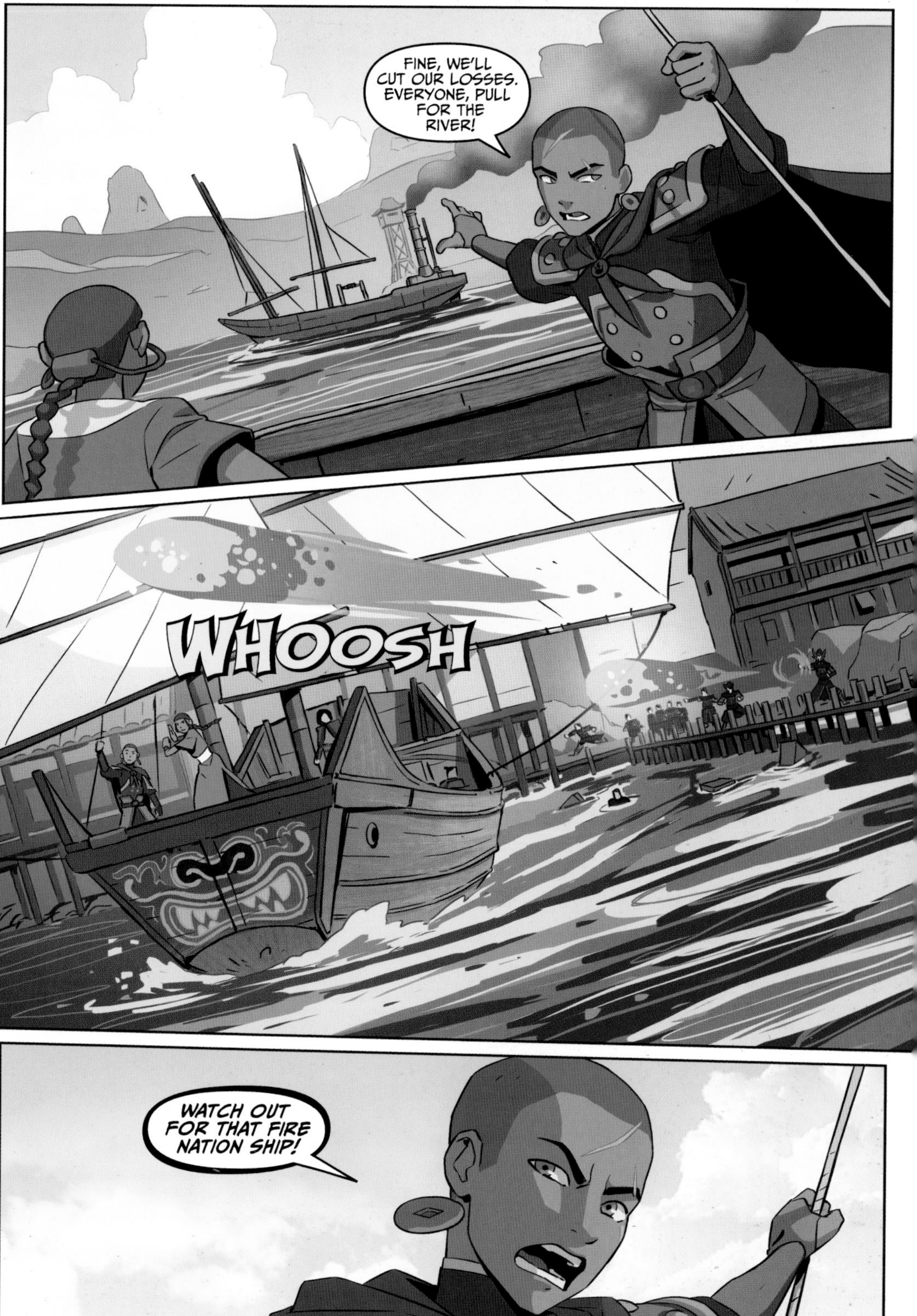
FINE, WE'LL CUT OUR LOSSES. EVERYONE, PULL FOR THE RIVER!
WHOOSH
WATCH OUT FOR THAT FIRE NATION SHIP!

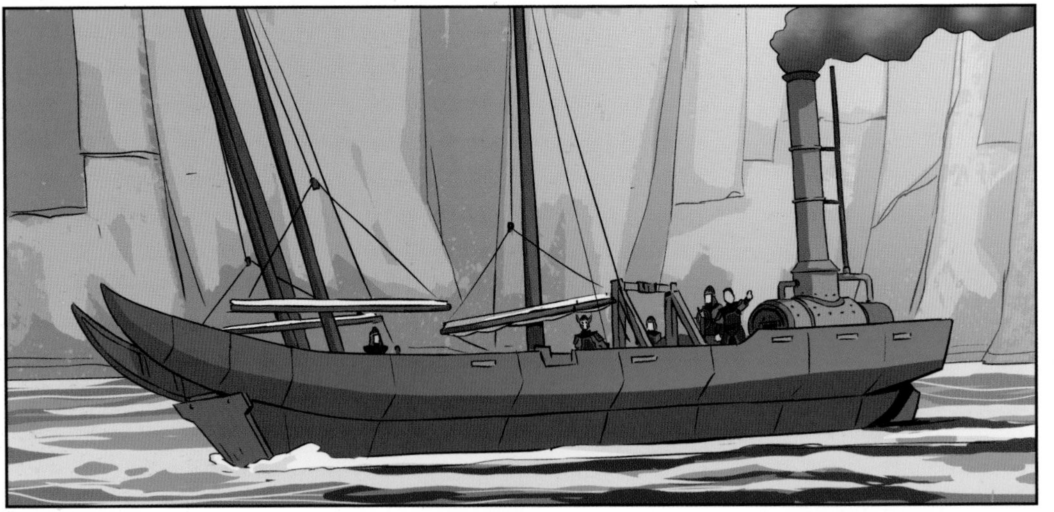

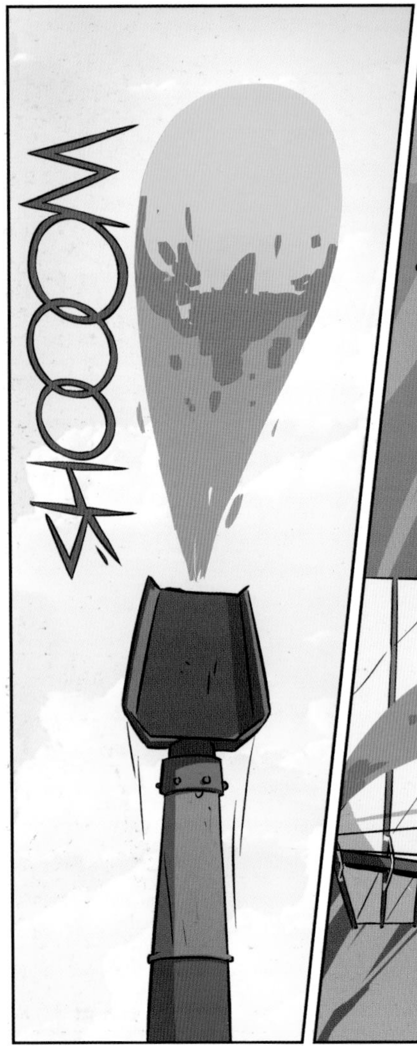
SHOOOM

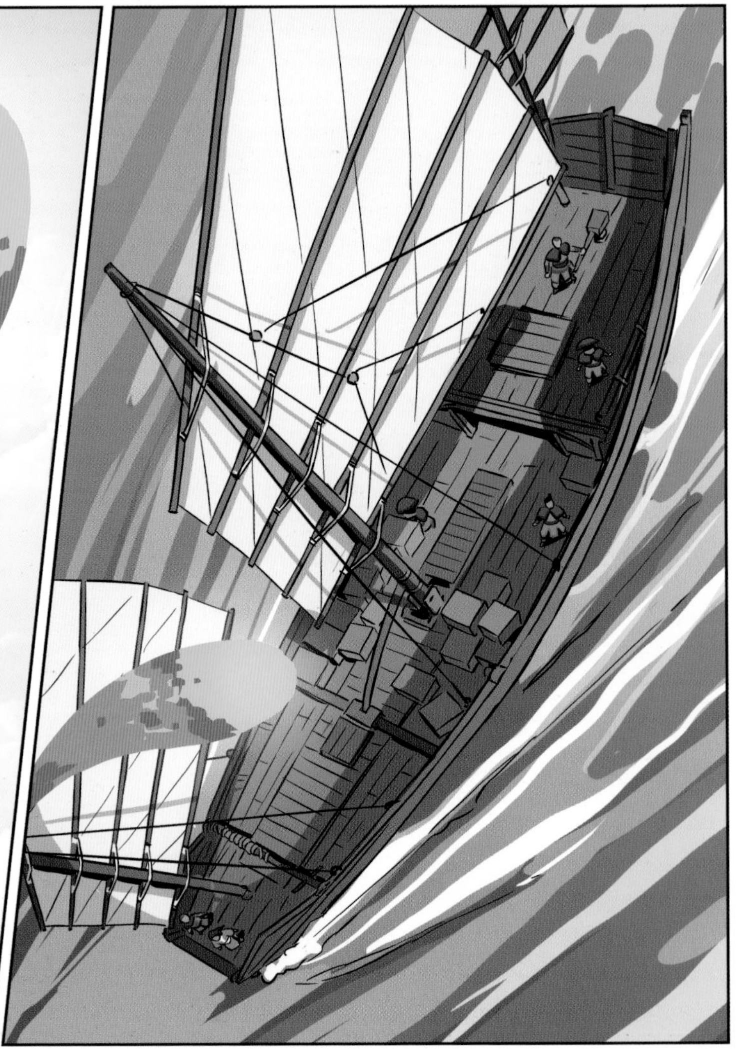

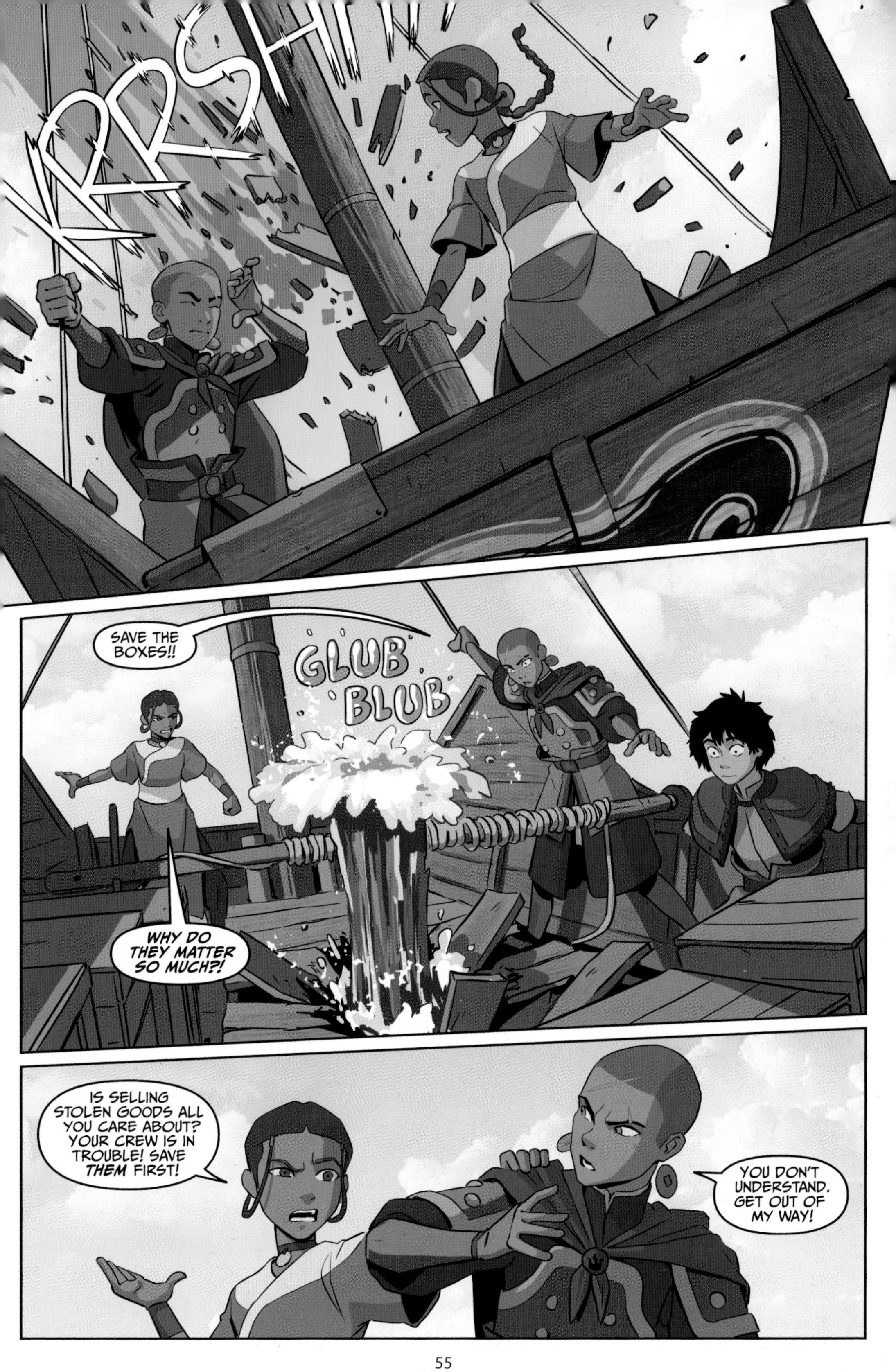
KRRSH!!
SAVE THE BOXES!!
GLUB BLUB
WHY DO THEY MATTER SO MUCH?!
IS SELLING STOLEN GOODS ALL YOU CARE ABOUT? YOUR CREW IS IN TROUBLE! SAVE *THEM* FIRST!
YOU DON'T UNDERSTAND. GET OUT OF MY WAY!

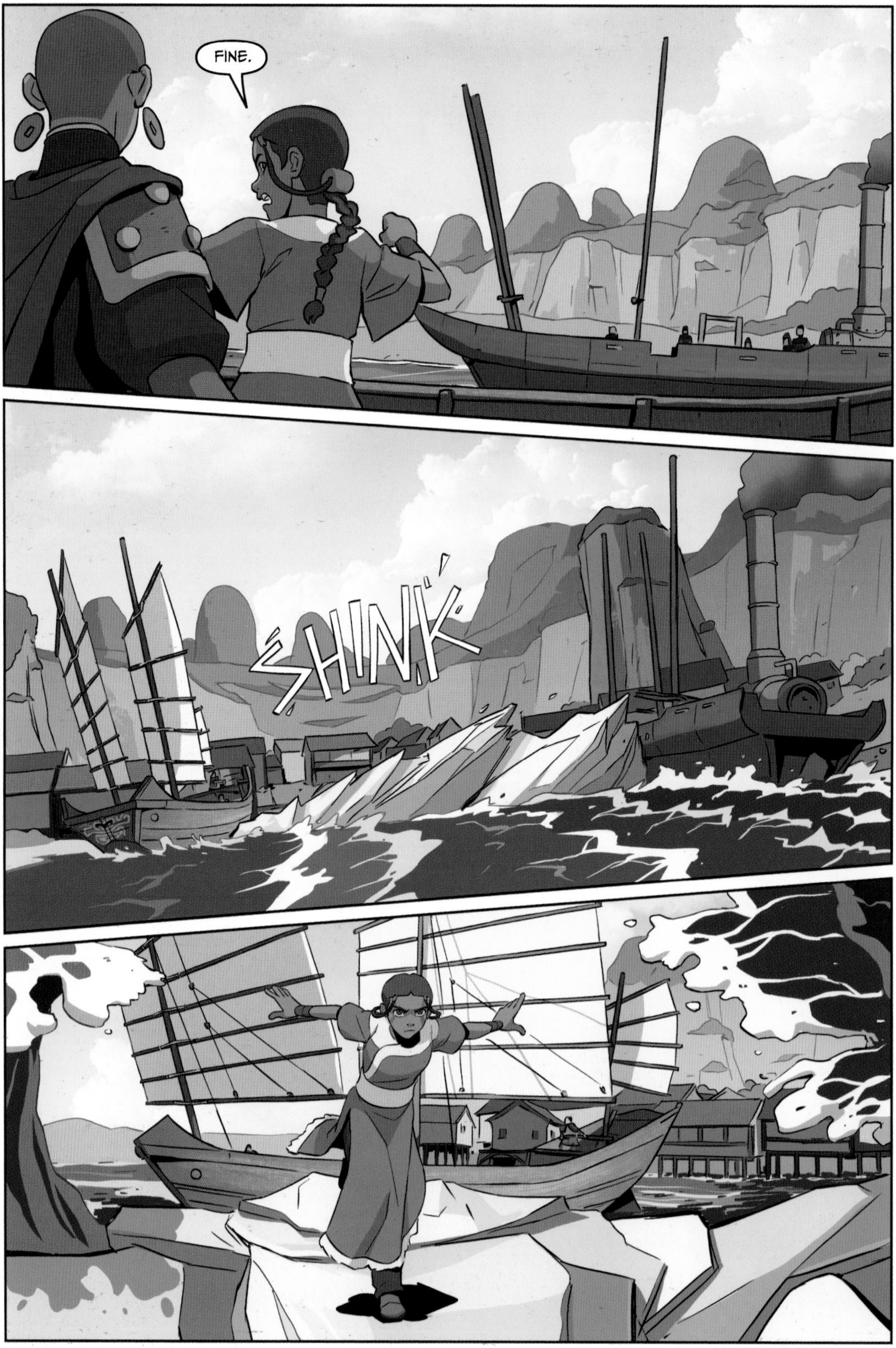
FINE.
SHINK

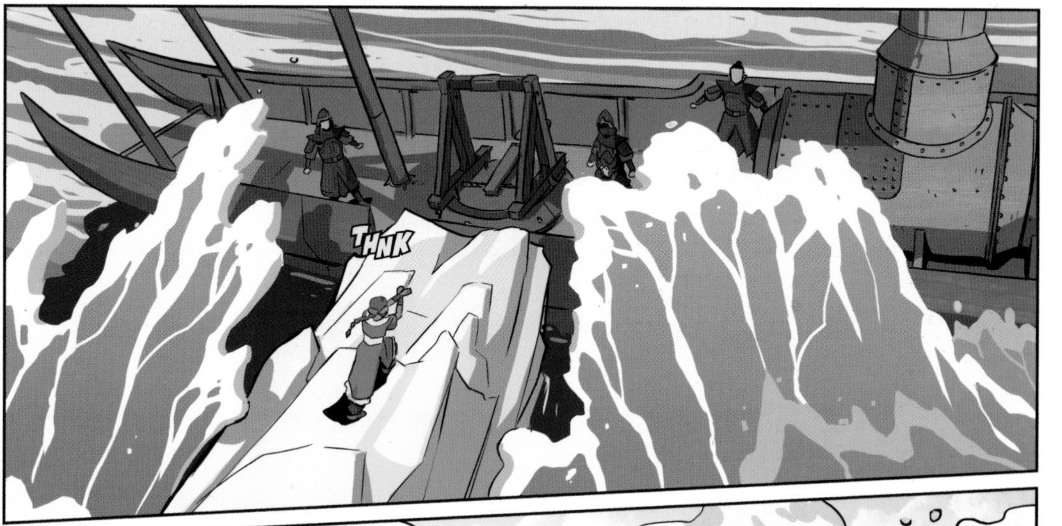
THNK

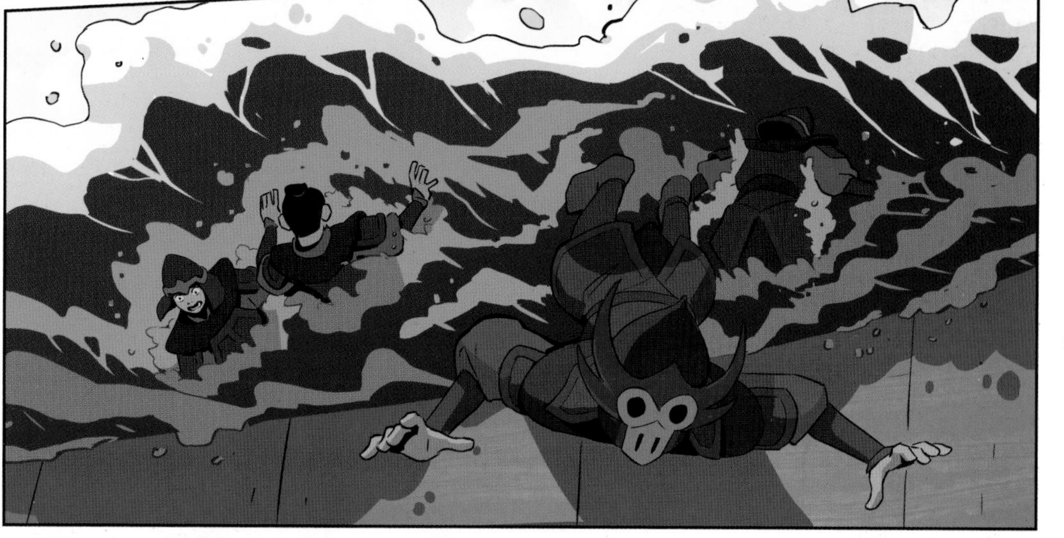

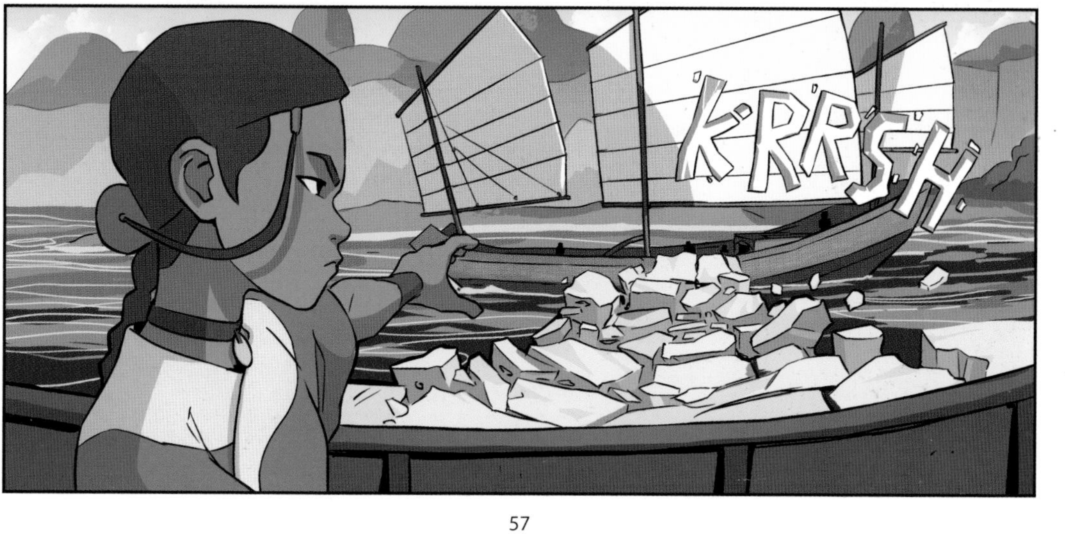
K-R-R-S-H

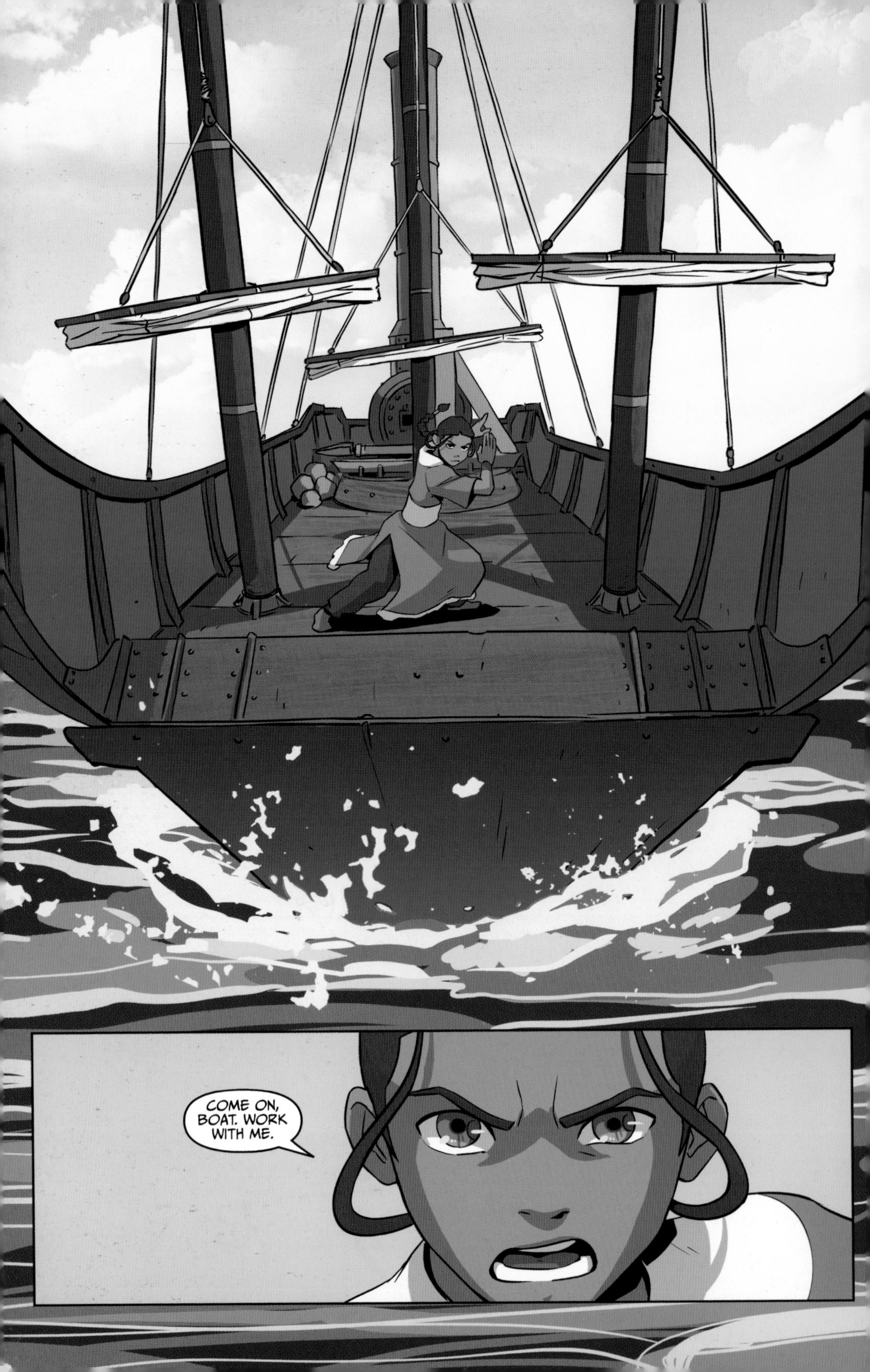
COME ON, BOAT. WORK WITH ME.

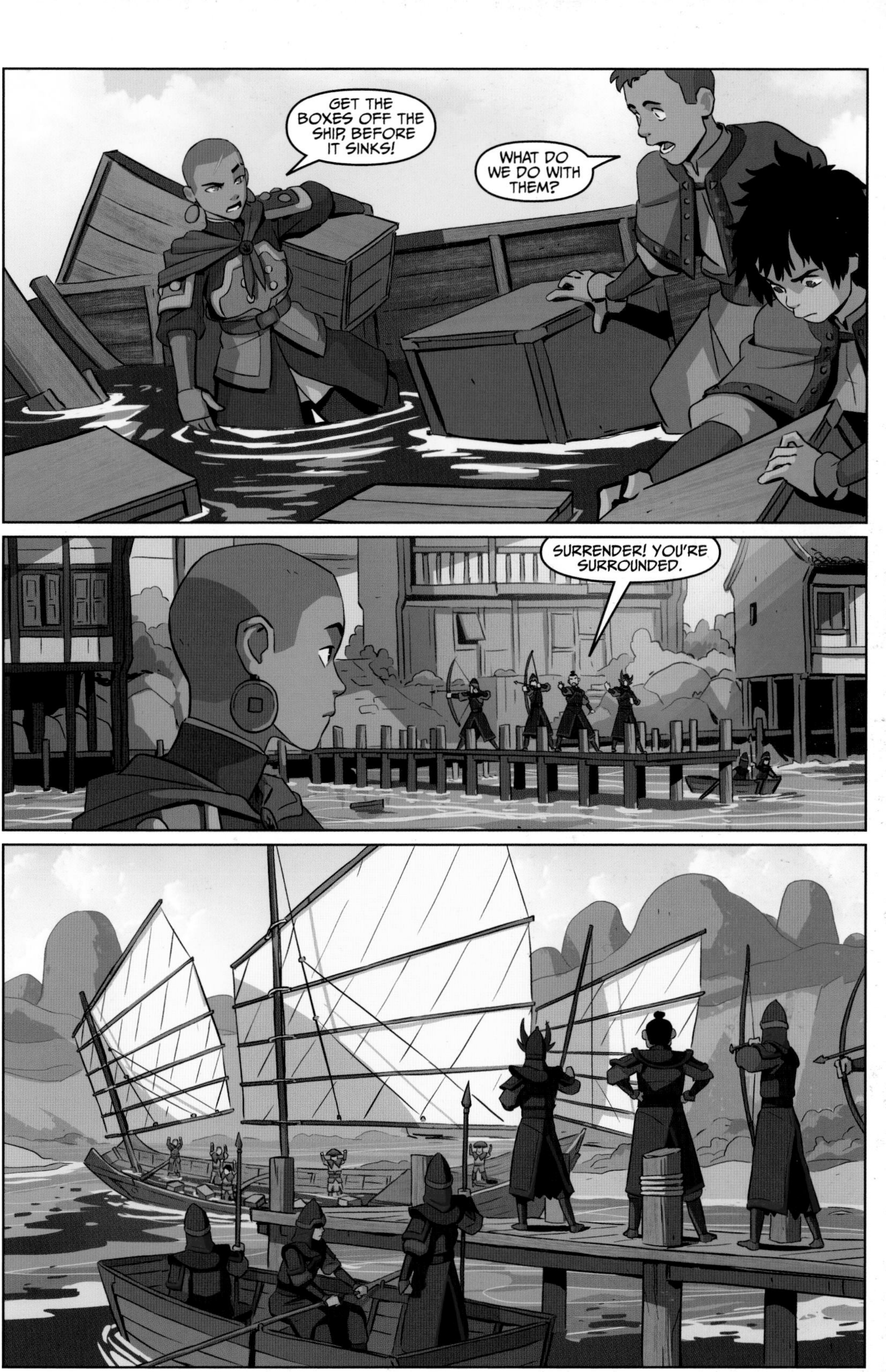
GET THE BOXES OFF THE SHIP, BEFORE IT SINKS!
WHAT DO WE DO WITH THEM?
SURRENDER! YOU'RE SURROUNDED.

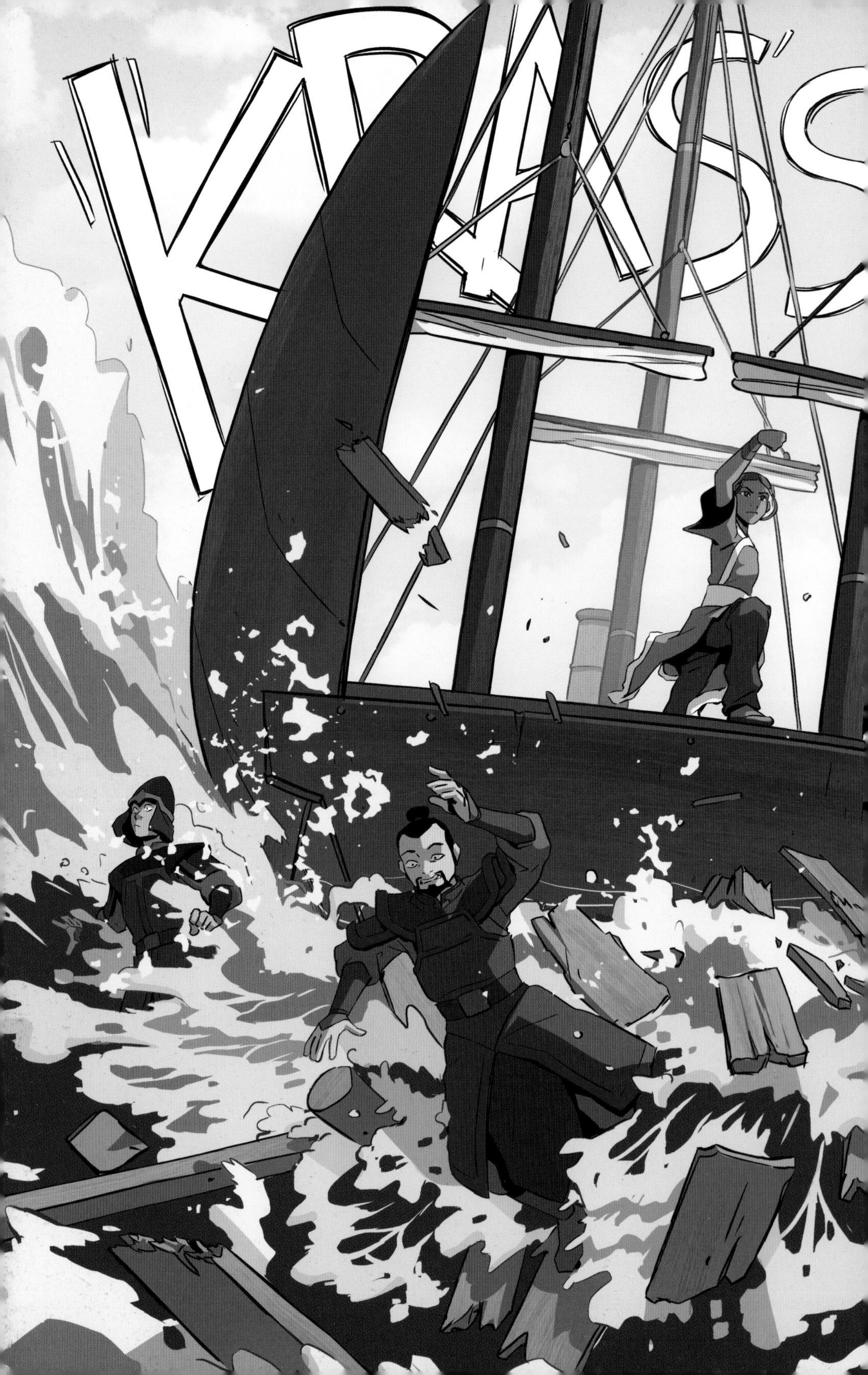
KRASS

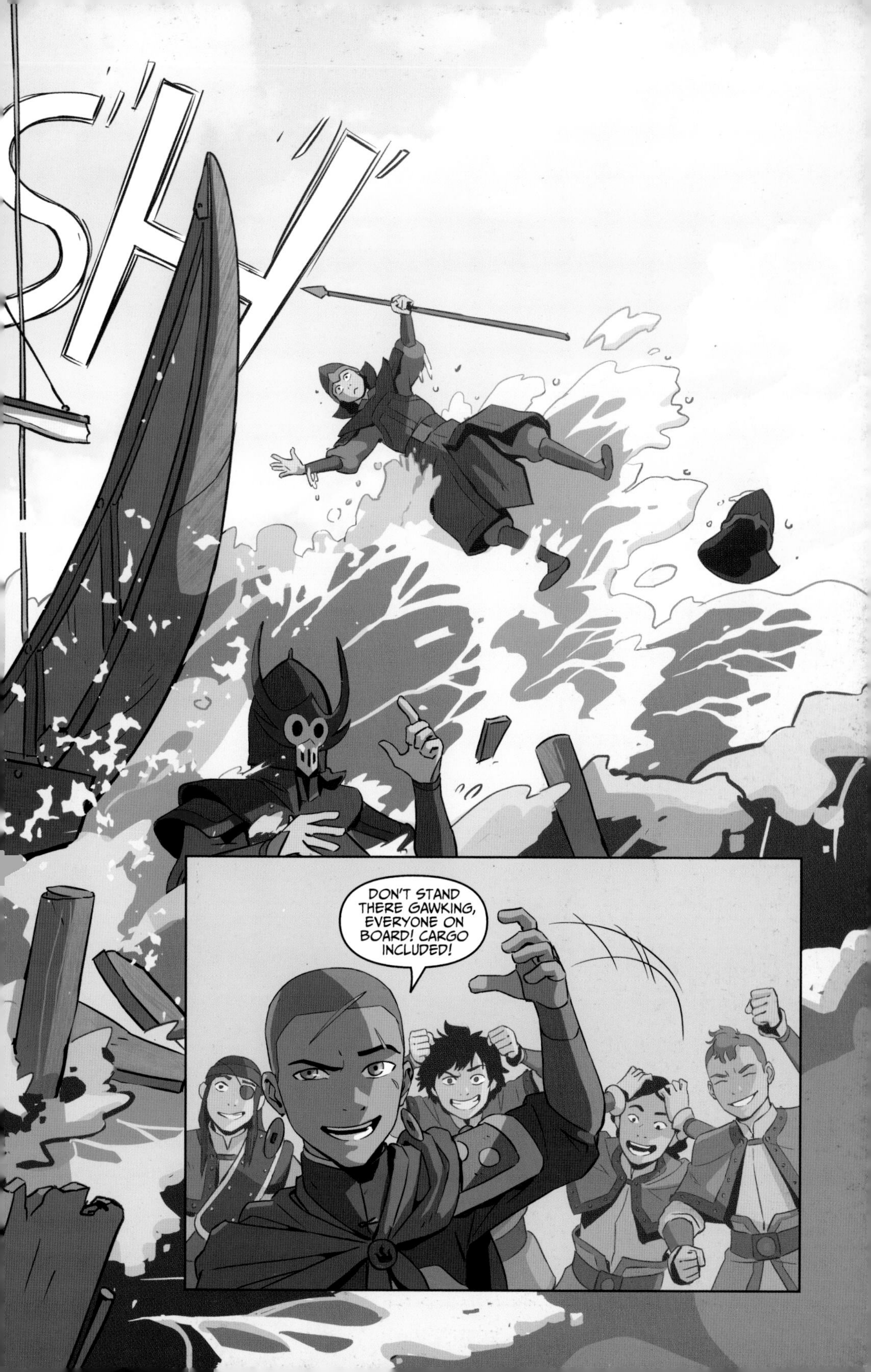
SHH
DON'T STAND THERE GAWKING, EVERYONE ON BOARD! CARGO INCLUDED!

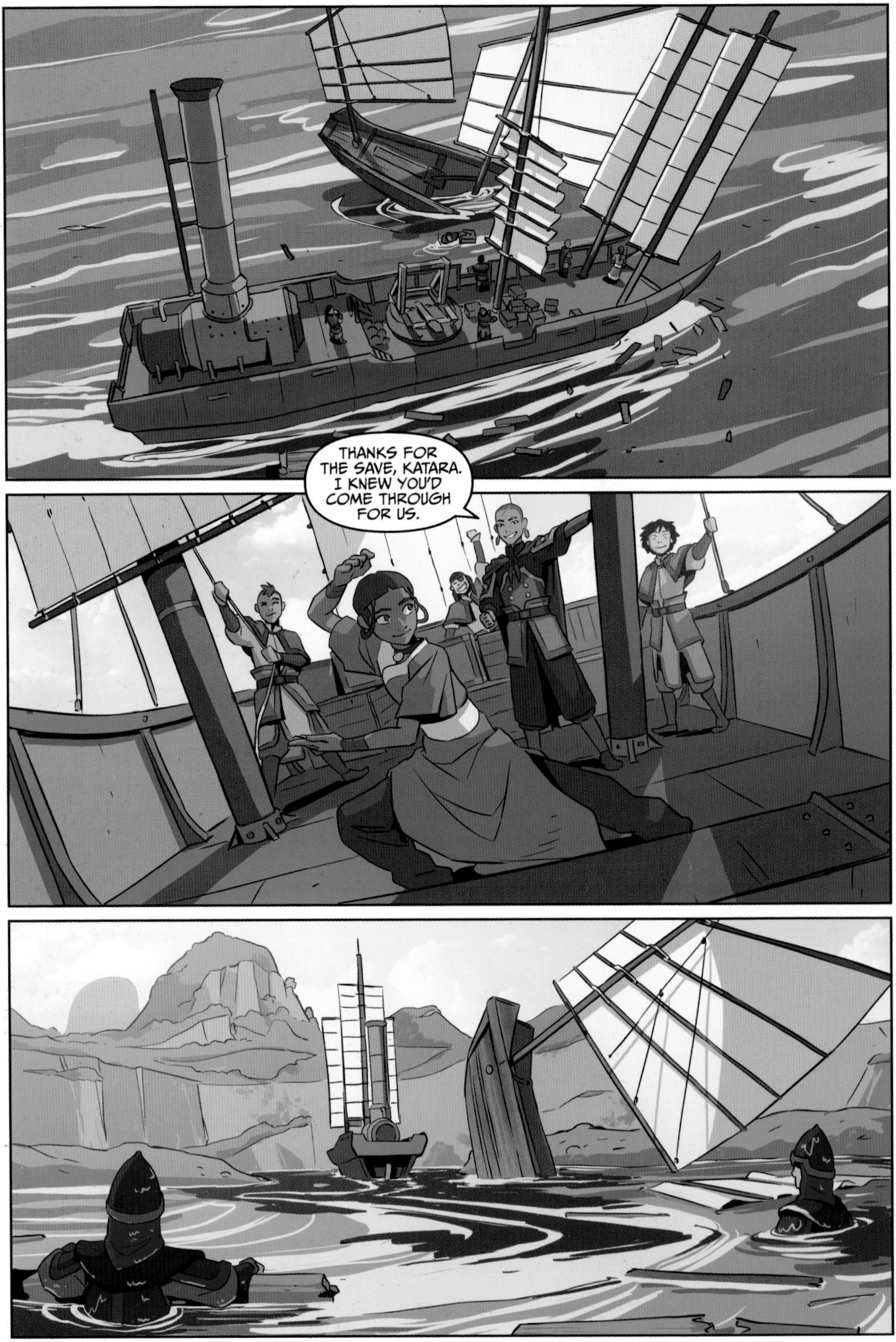
THANKS FOR THE SAVE, KATARA. I KNEW YOU'D COME THROUGH FOR US.

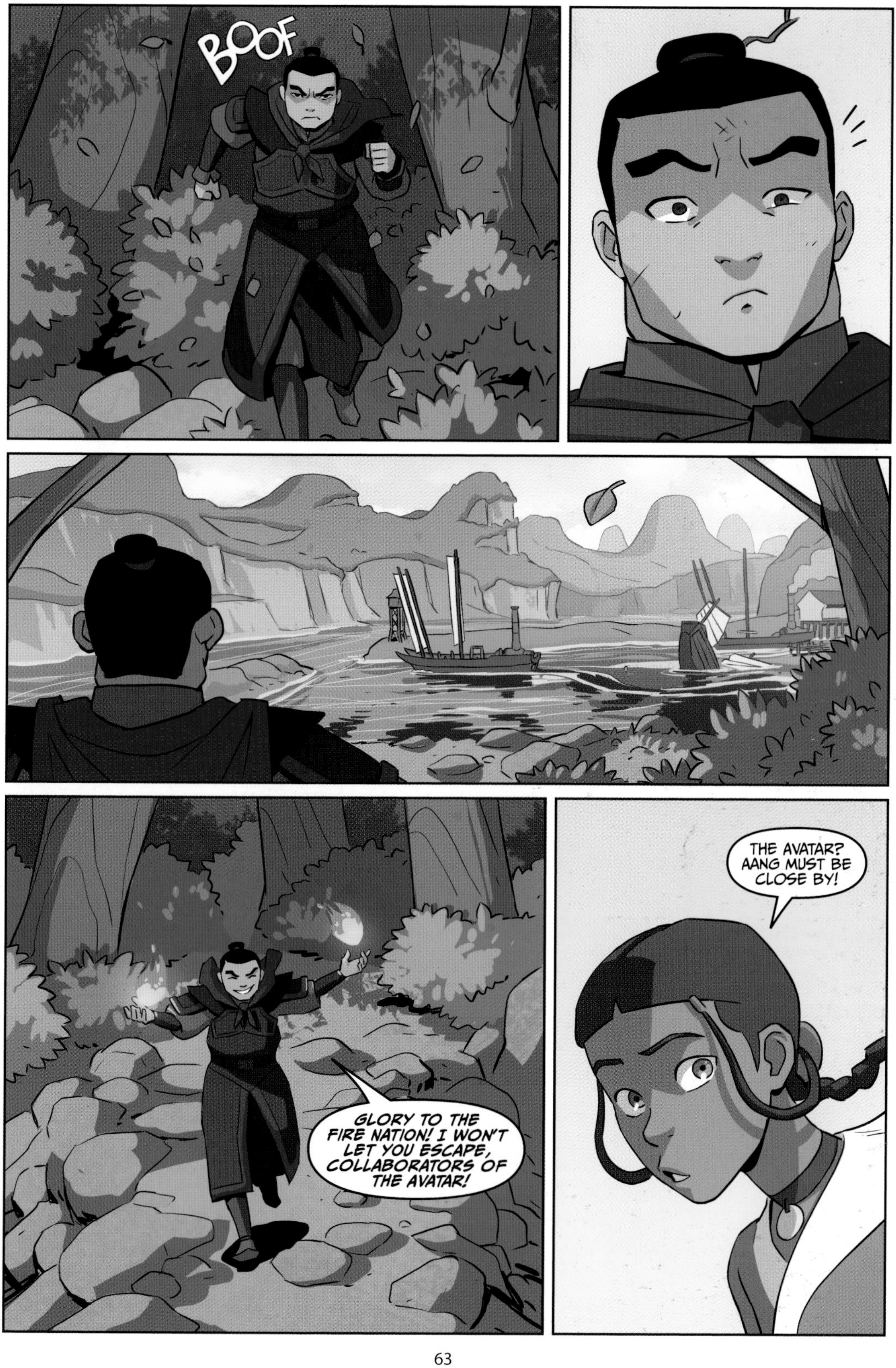
BOOF
GLORY TO THE FIRE NATION! I WON'T LET YOU ESCAPE, COLLABORATORS OF THE AVATAR!
THE AVATAR? AANG MUST BE CLOSE BY!

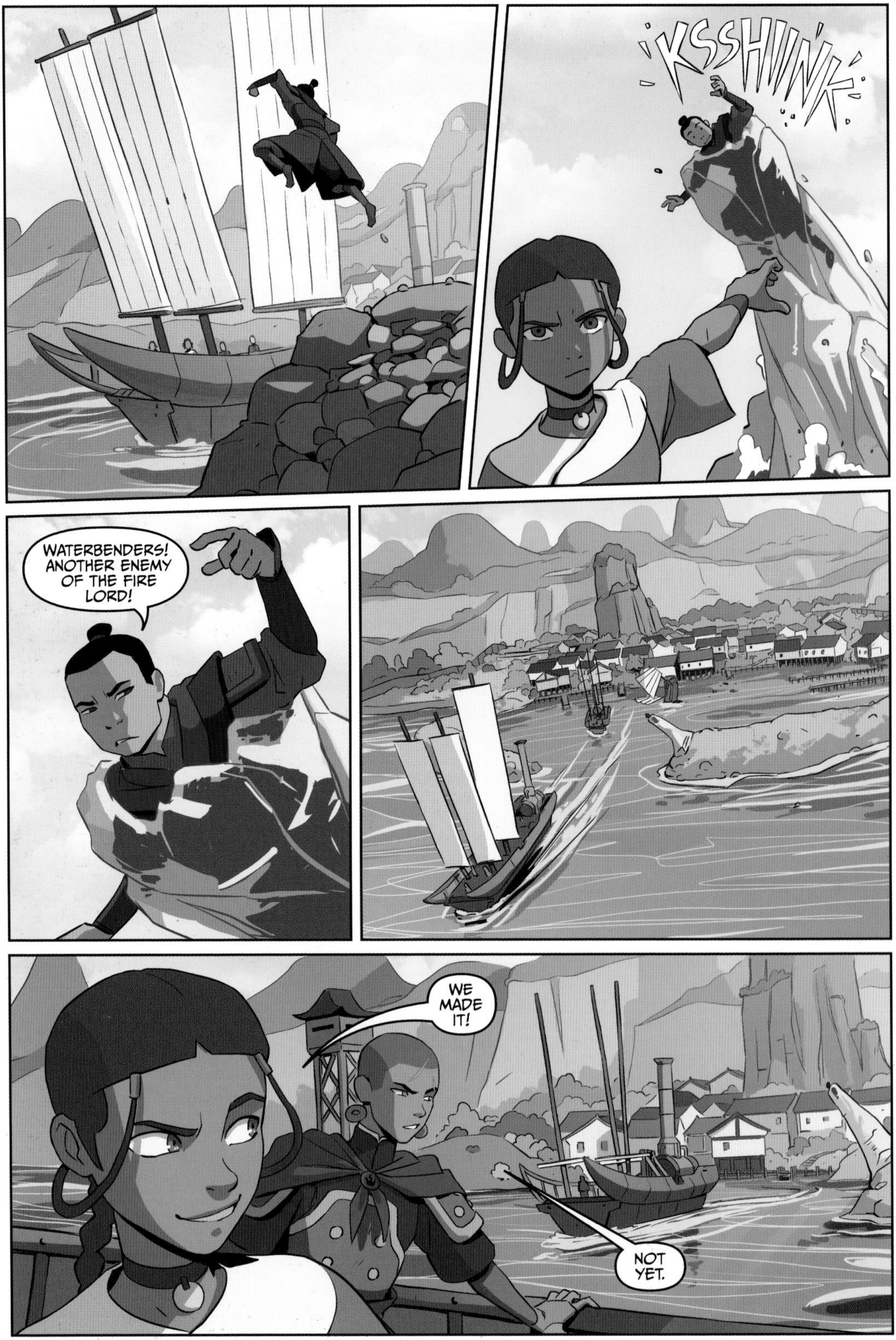
KSSHIINK
WATERBENDERS! ANOTHER ENEMY OF THE FIRE LORD!
WE MADE IT!
NOT YET.

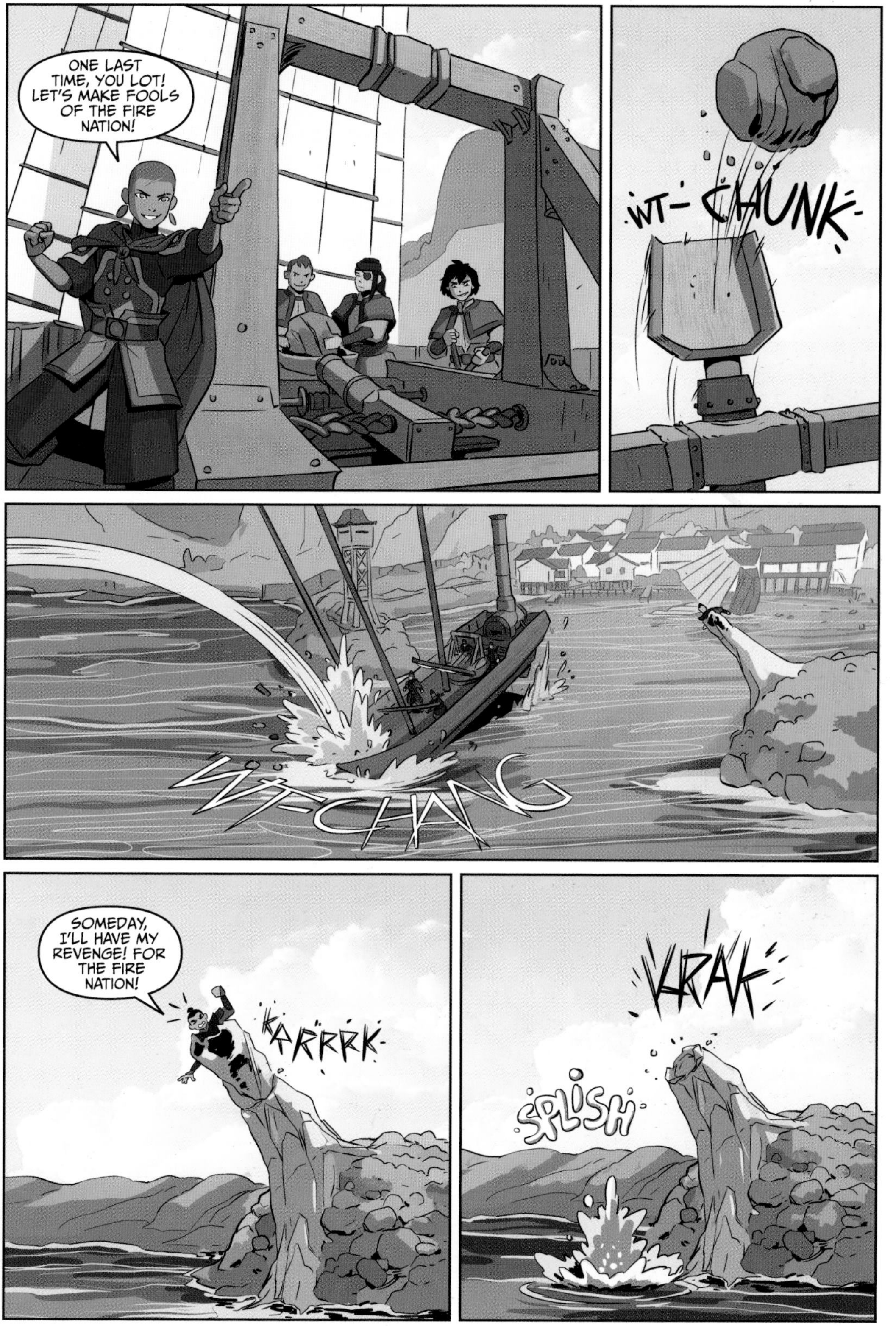
ONE LAST TIME, YOU LOT! LET'S MAKE FOOLS OF THE FIRE NATION!
WT-CHUNK
WTCHANG
SOMEDAY, I'LL HAVE MY REVENGE! FOR THE FIRE NATION!
KRRRRK
KRAK
SPLISH

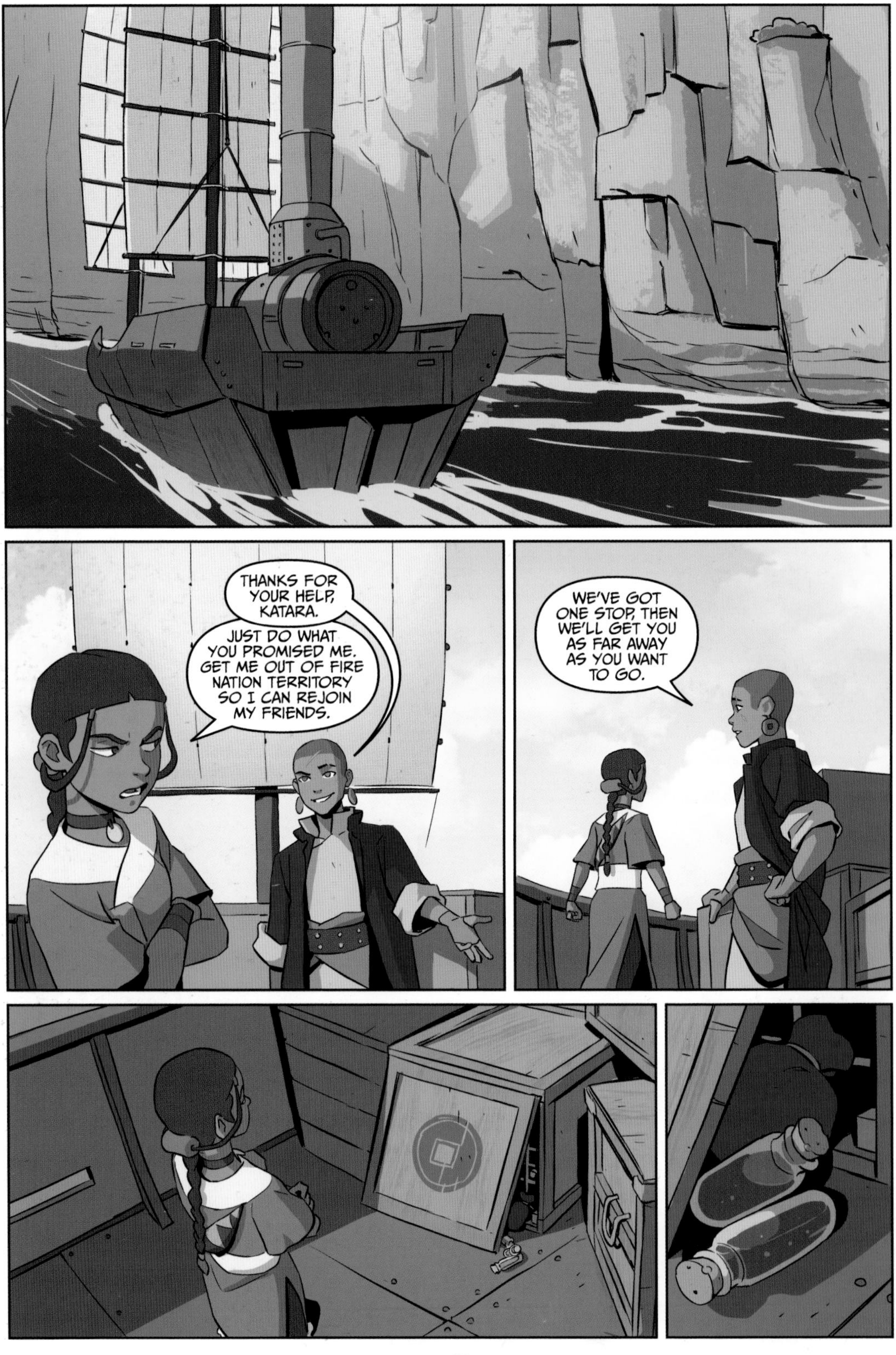
THANKS FOR YOUR HELP, KATARA.
JUST DO WHAT YOU PROMISED ME. GET ME OUT OF FIRE NATION TERRITORY SO I CAN REJOIN MY FRIENDS.
WE'VE GOT ONE STOP, THEN WE'LL GET YOU AS FAR AWAY AS YOU WANT TO GO.

THIS ISN'T CONTRABAND. THIS IS MEDICINE.

I USED TO HELP MY GRAN GRAN PREPARE THESE HERBS ALL THE TIME BACK AT THE SOUTHERN WATER TRIBE.

YOU'RE EVEN WORSE THAN I THOUGHT. YOU'RE GOING TO MAKE SICK PEOPLE PAY FOR THIS MEDICINE! HOW COULD YOU BE SO CRUEL?

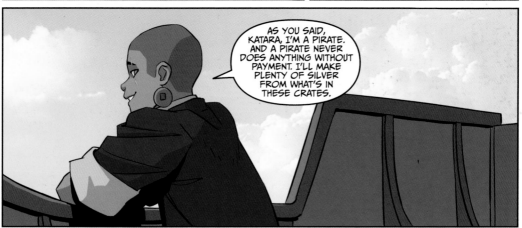

AS YOU SAID, KATARA, I'M A PIRATE. AND A PIRATE NEVER DOES ANYTHING WITHOUT PAYMENT. I'LL MAKE PLENTY OF SILVER FROM WHAT'S IN THESE CRATES.

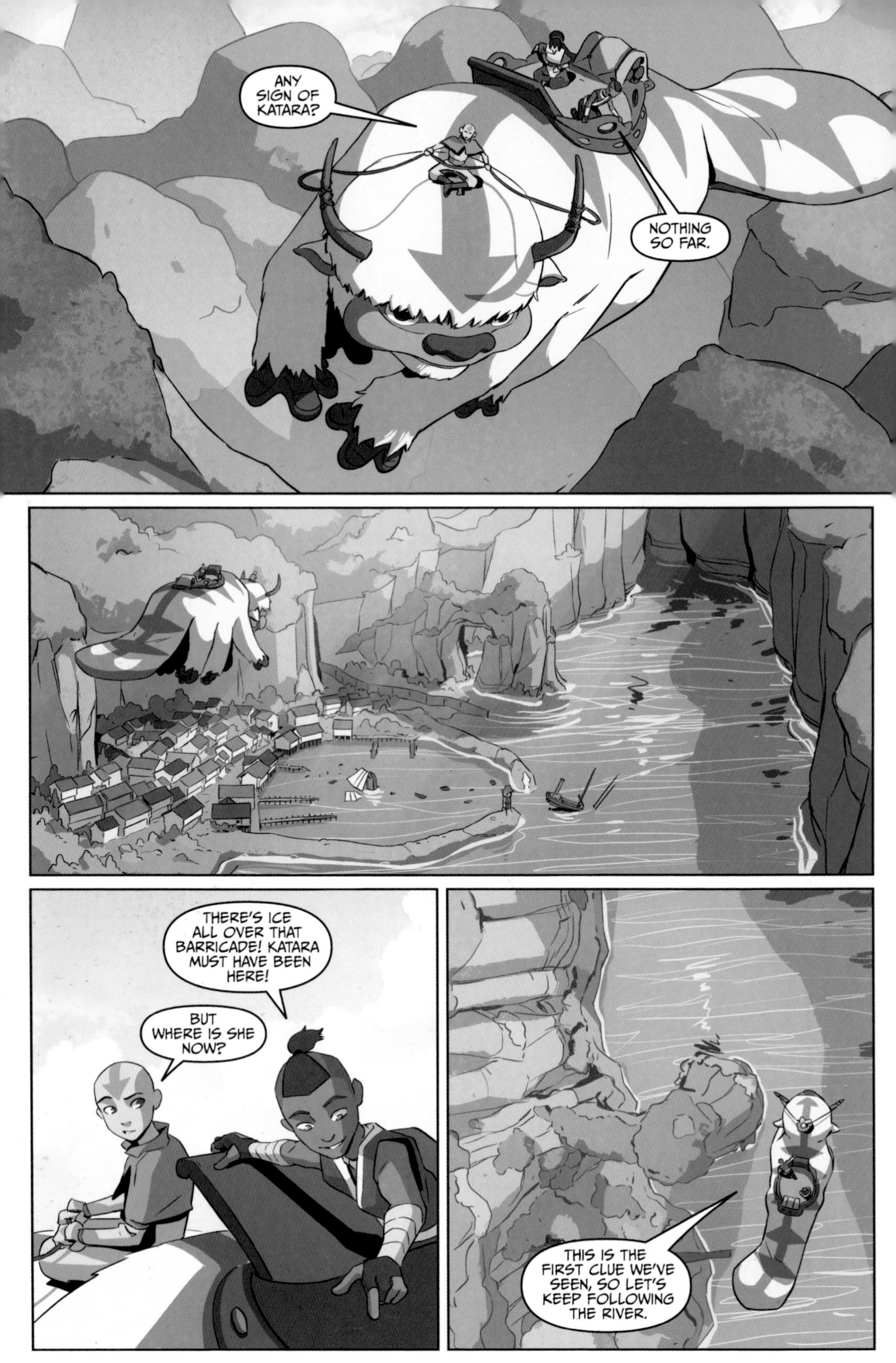
ANY SIGN OF KATARA?
NOTHING SO FAR.
THERE'S ICE ALL OVER THAT BARRICADE! KATARA MUST HAVE BEEN HERE!
BUT WHERE IS SHE NOW?
THIS IS THE FIRST CLUE WE'VE SEEN, SO LET'S KEEP FOLLOWING THE RIVER.

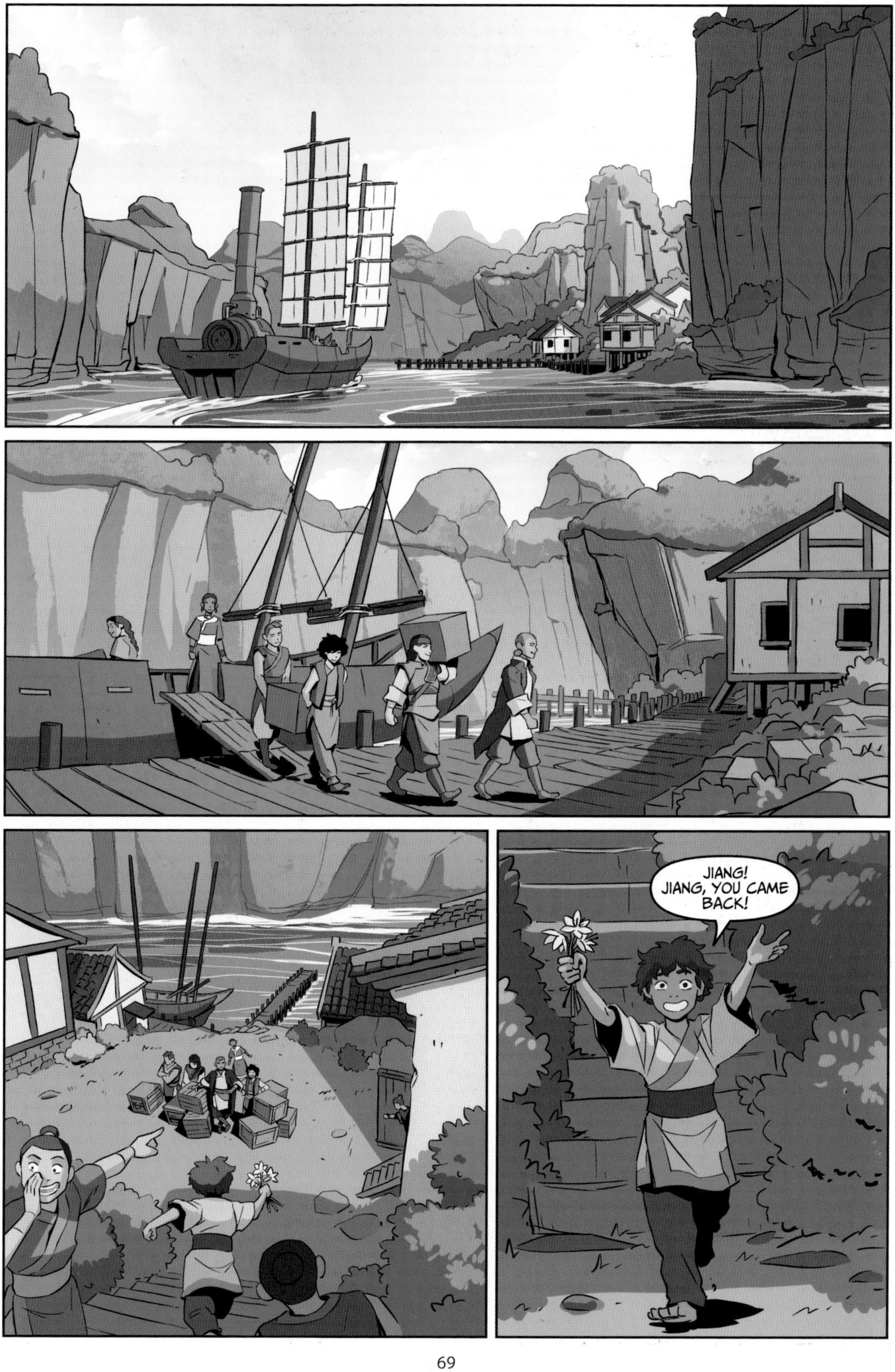
JIANG! JIANG, YOU CAME BACK!

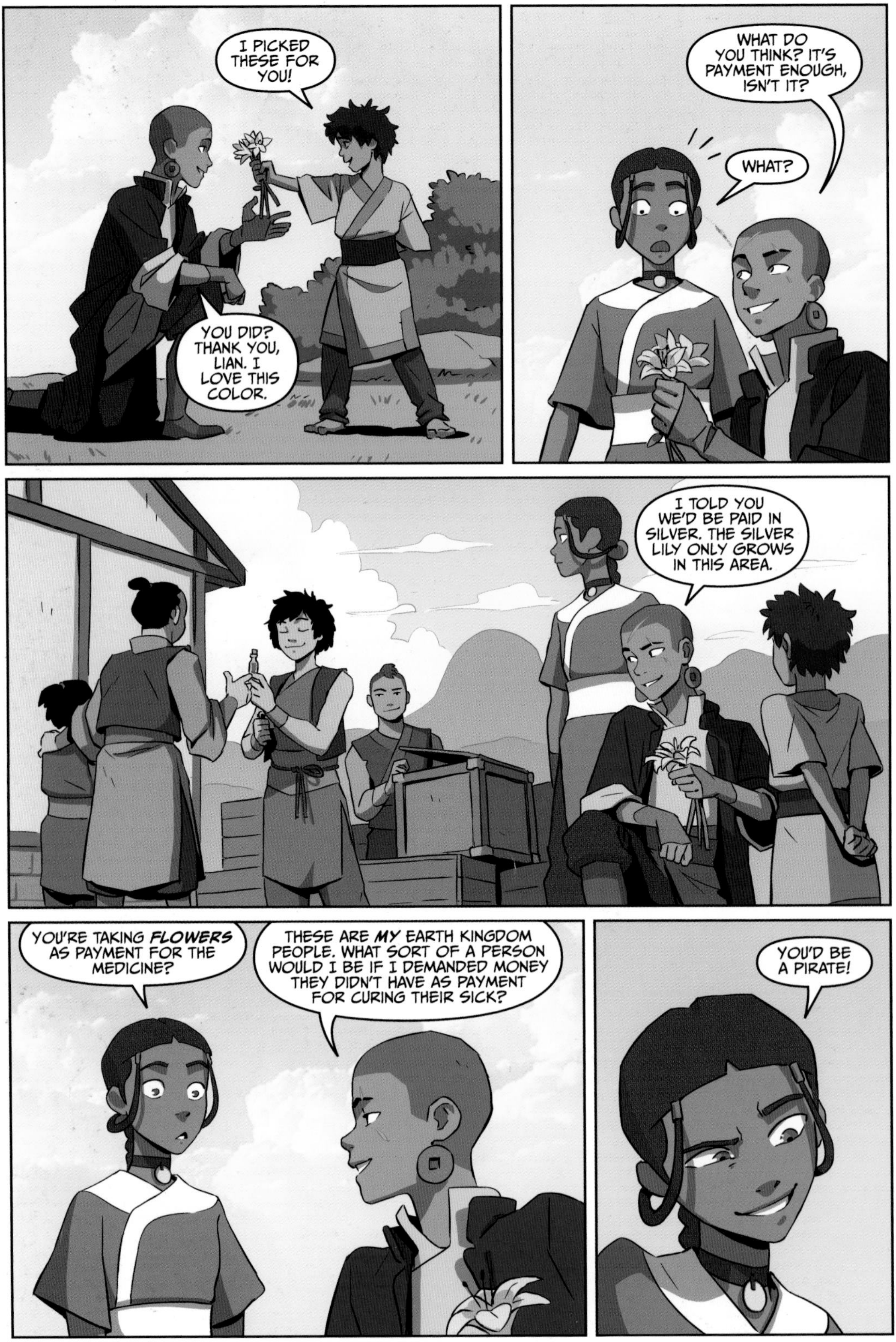

I PICKED THESE FOR YOU!
YOU DID? THANK YOU, LIAN. I LOVE THIS COLOR.
WHAT DO YOU THINK? IT'S PAYMENT ENOUGH, ISN'T IT?
WHAT?
I TOLD YOU WE'D BE PAID IN SILVER. THE SILVER LILY ONLY GROWS IN THIS AREA.
YOU'RE TAKING ***FLOWERS*** AS PAYMENT FOR THE MEDICINE?
THESE ARE ***MY*** EARTH KINGDOM PEOPLE. WHAT SORT OF A PERSON WOULD I BE IF I DEMANDED MONEY THEY DIDN'T HAVE AS PAYMENT FOR CURING THEIR SICK?
YOU'D BE A PIRATE!

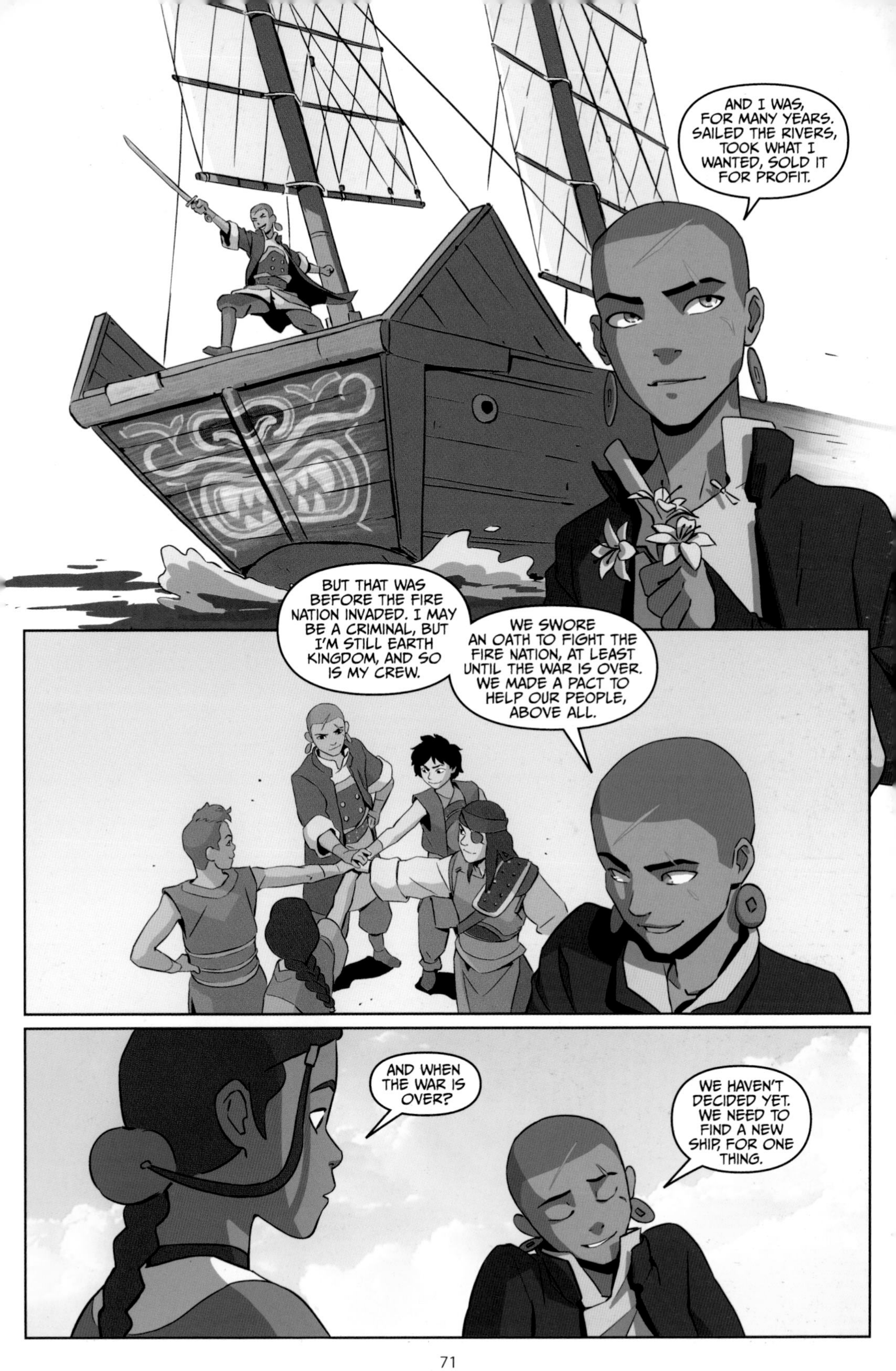
AND I WAS, FOR MANY YEARS. SAILED THE RIVERS, TOOK WHAT I WANTED, SOLD IT FOR PROFIT.
BUT THAT WAS BEFORE THE FIRE NATION INVADED. I MAY BE A CRIMINAL, BUT I'M STILL EARTH KINGDOM, AND SO IS MY CREW.
WE SWORE AN OATH TO FIGHT THE FIRE NATION, AT LEAST UNTIL THE WAR IS OVER. WE MADE A PACT TO HELP OUR PEOPLE, ABOVE ALL.
AND WHEN THE WAR IS OVER?
WE HAVEN'T DECIDED YET. WE NEED TO FIND A NEW SHIP, FOR ONE THING.

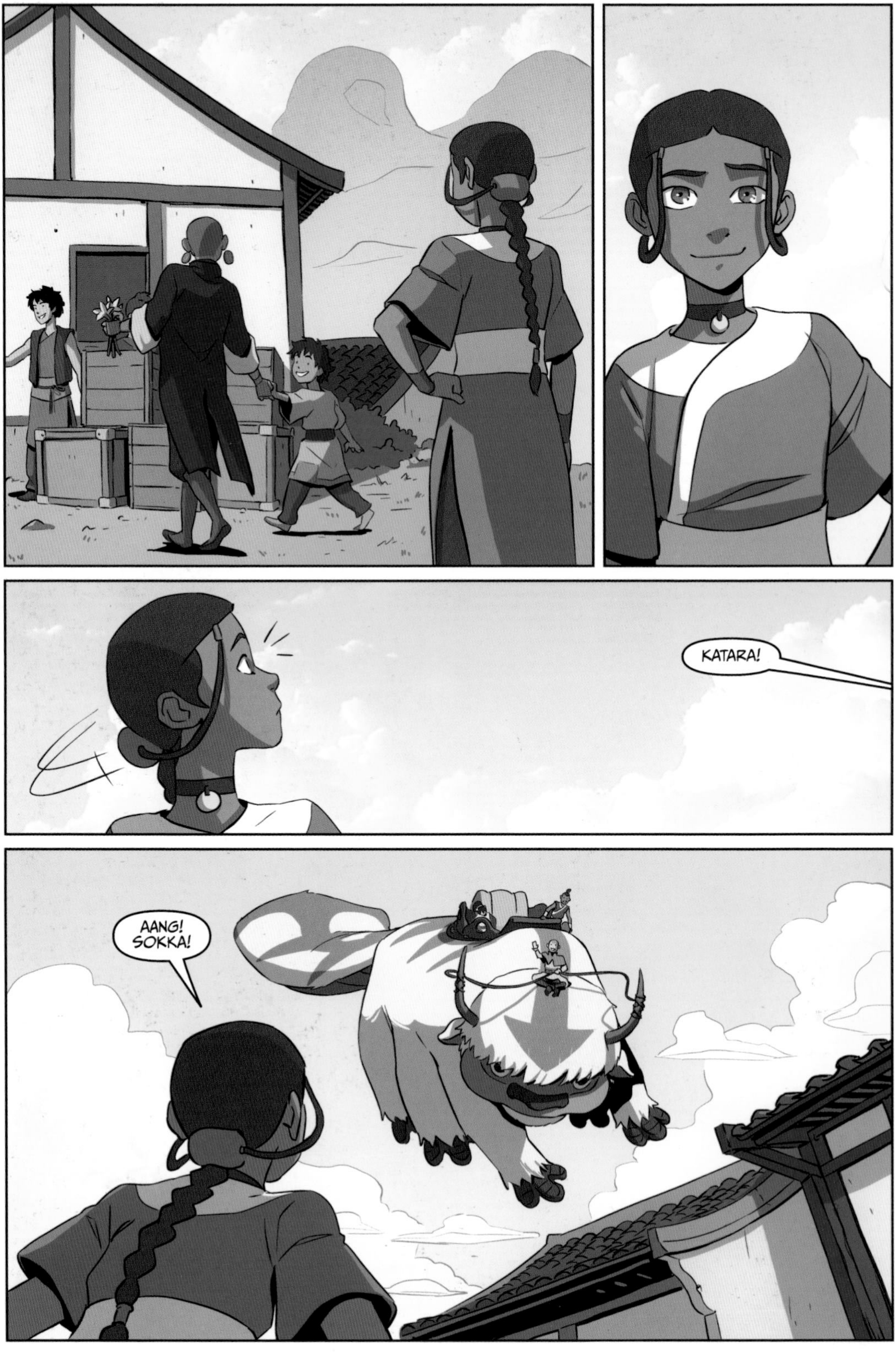
KATARA!
AANG! SOKKA!

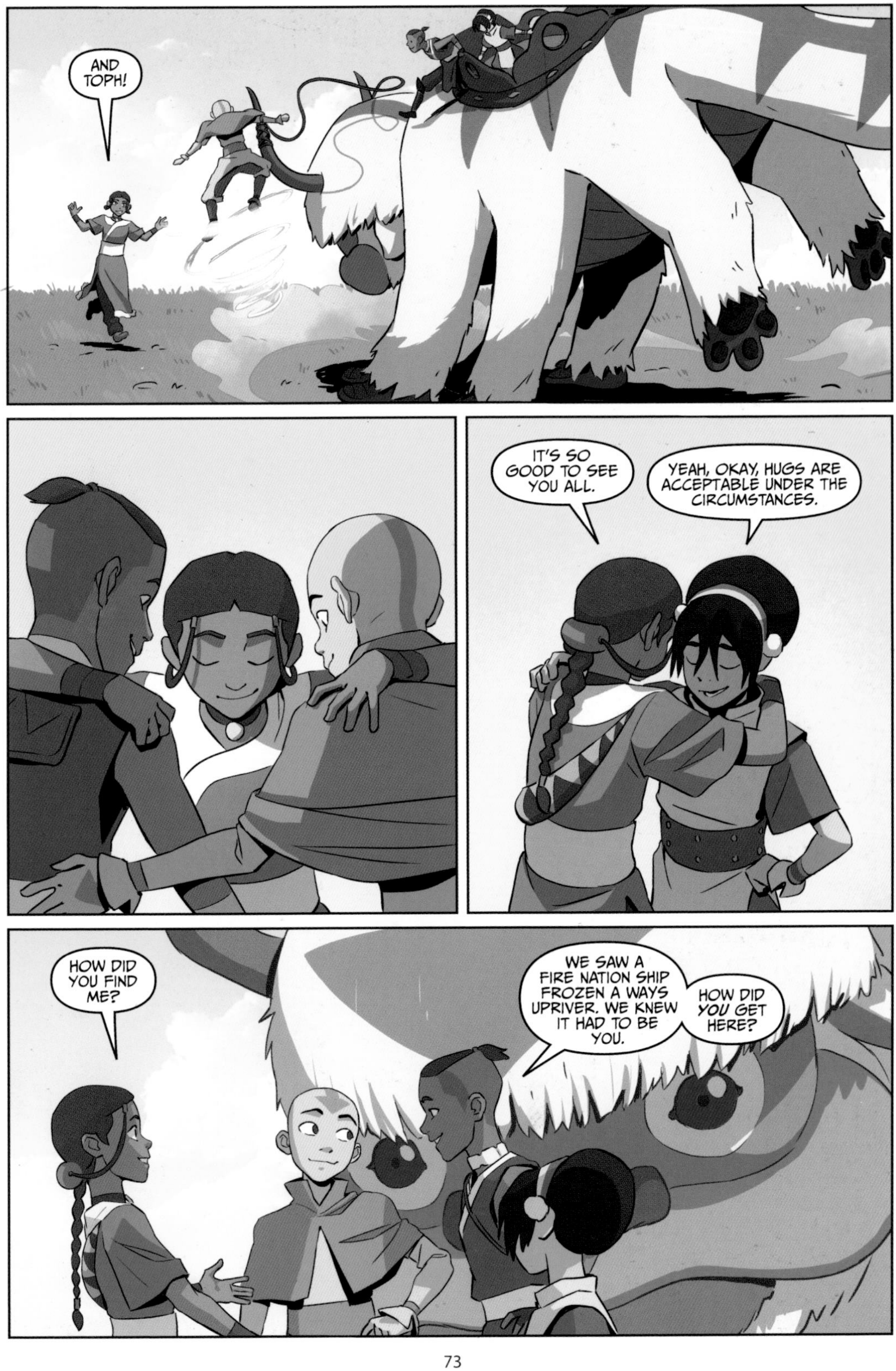
AND TOPH!
IT'S SO GOOD TO SEE YOU ALL.
YEAH, OKAY, HUGS ARE ACCEPTABLE UNDER THE CIRCUMSTANCES.
HOW DID YOU FIND ME?
WE SAW A FIRE NATION SHIP FROZEN A WAYS UPRIVER. WE KNEW IT HAD TO BE YOU.
HOW DID *YOU* GET HERE?

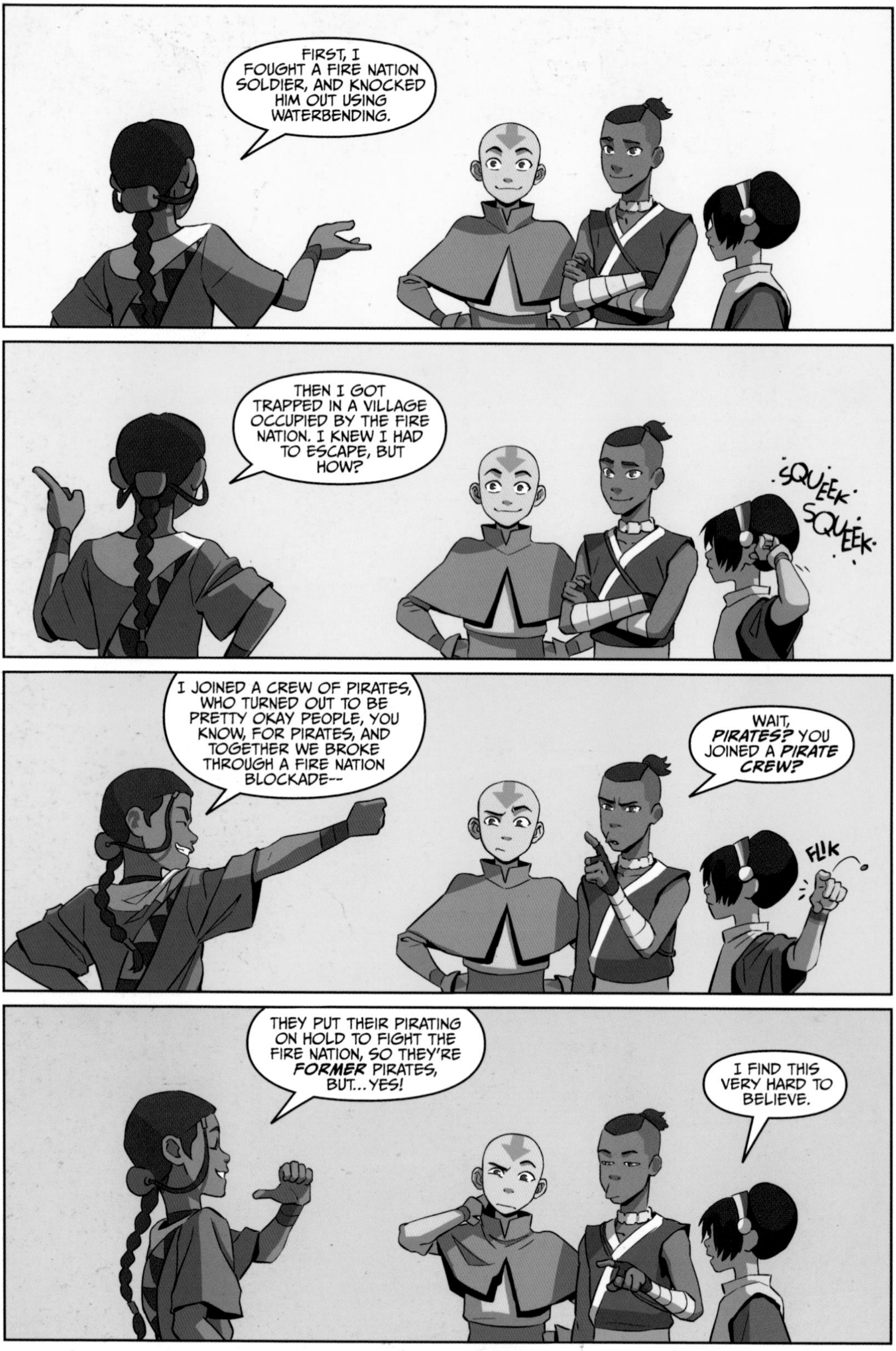
FIRST, I FOUGHT A FIRE NATION SOLDIER, AND KNOCKED HIM OUT USING WATERBENDING.
THEN I GOT TRAPPED IN A VILLAGE OCCUPIED BY THE FIRE NATION. I KNEW I HAD TO ESCAPE, BUT HOW?
SQUEEK SQUEEK
I JOINED A CREW OF PIRATES, WHO TURNED OUT TO BE PRETTY OKAY PEOPLE, YOU KNOW, FOR PIRATES, AND TOGETHER WE BROKE THROUGH A FIRE NATION BLOCKADE--
WAIT, PIRATES? YOU JOINED A PIRATE CREW?
FLIK
THEY PUT THEIR PIRATING ON HOLD TO FIGHT THE FIRE NATION, SO THEY'RE FORMER PIRATES, BUT...YES!
I FIND THIS VERY HARD TO BELIEVE.

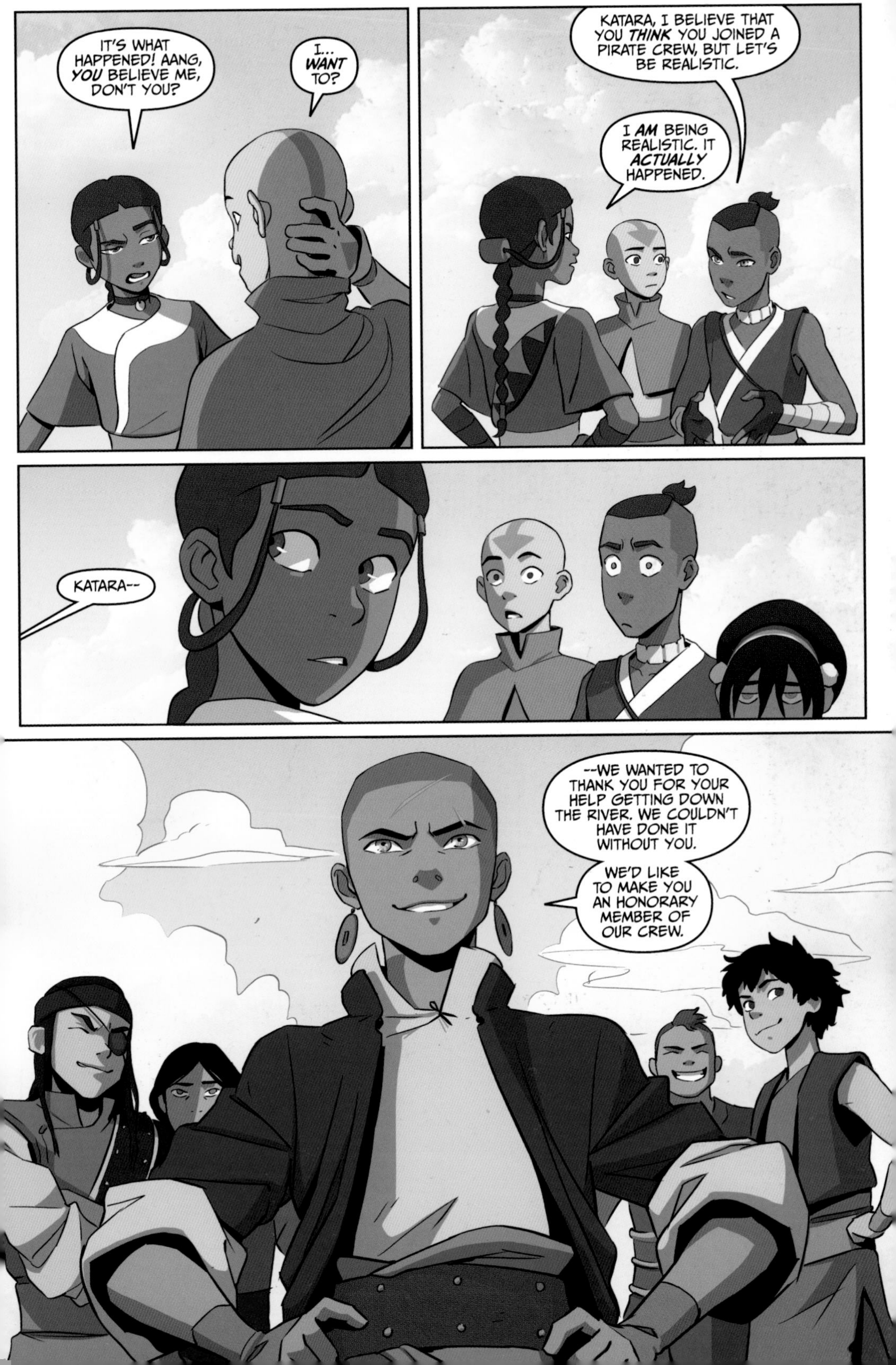
IT'S WHAT HAPPENED! AANG, *YOU* BELIEVE ME, DON'T YOU?
I... *WANT* TO?
KATARA, I BELIEVE THAT YOU *THINK* YOU JOINED A PIRATE CREW, BUT LET'S BE REALISTIC.
I *AM* BEING REALISTIC. IT *ACTUALLY* HAPPENED.
KATARA--
--WE WANTED TO THANK YOU FOR YOUR HELP GETTING DOWN THE RIVER. WE COULDN'T HAVE DONE IT WITHOUT YOU.
WE'D LIKE TO MAKE YOU AN HONORARY MEMBER OF OUR CREW.

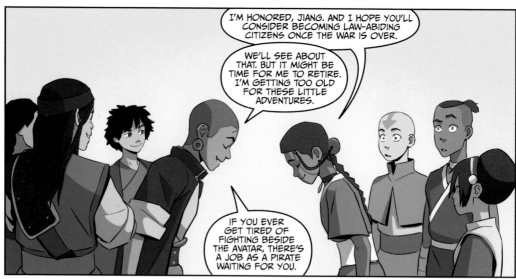

I'M HONORED, JIANG. AND I HOPE YOU'LL CONSIDER BECOMING LAW-ABIDING CITIZENS ONCE THE WAR IS OVER.

WE'LL SEE ABOUT THAT. BUT IT MIGHT BE TIME FOR ME TO RETIRE. I'M GETTING TOO OLD FOR THESE LITTLE ADVENTURES.

IF YOU EVER GET TIRED OF FIGHTING BESIDE THE AVATAR, THERE'S A JOB AS A PIRATE WAITING FOR YOU.

YOU WERE SAYING?

I WAS JUST SAYING YOU'RE THE *COOLEST* SISTER IN THE WORLD.

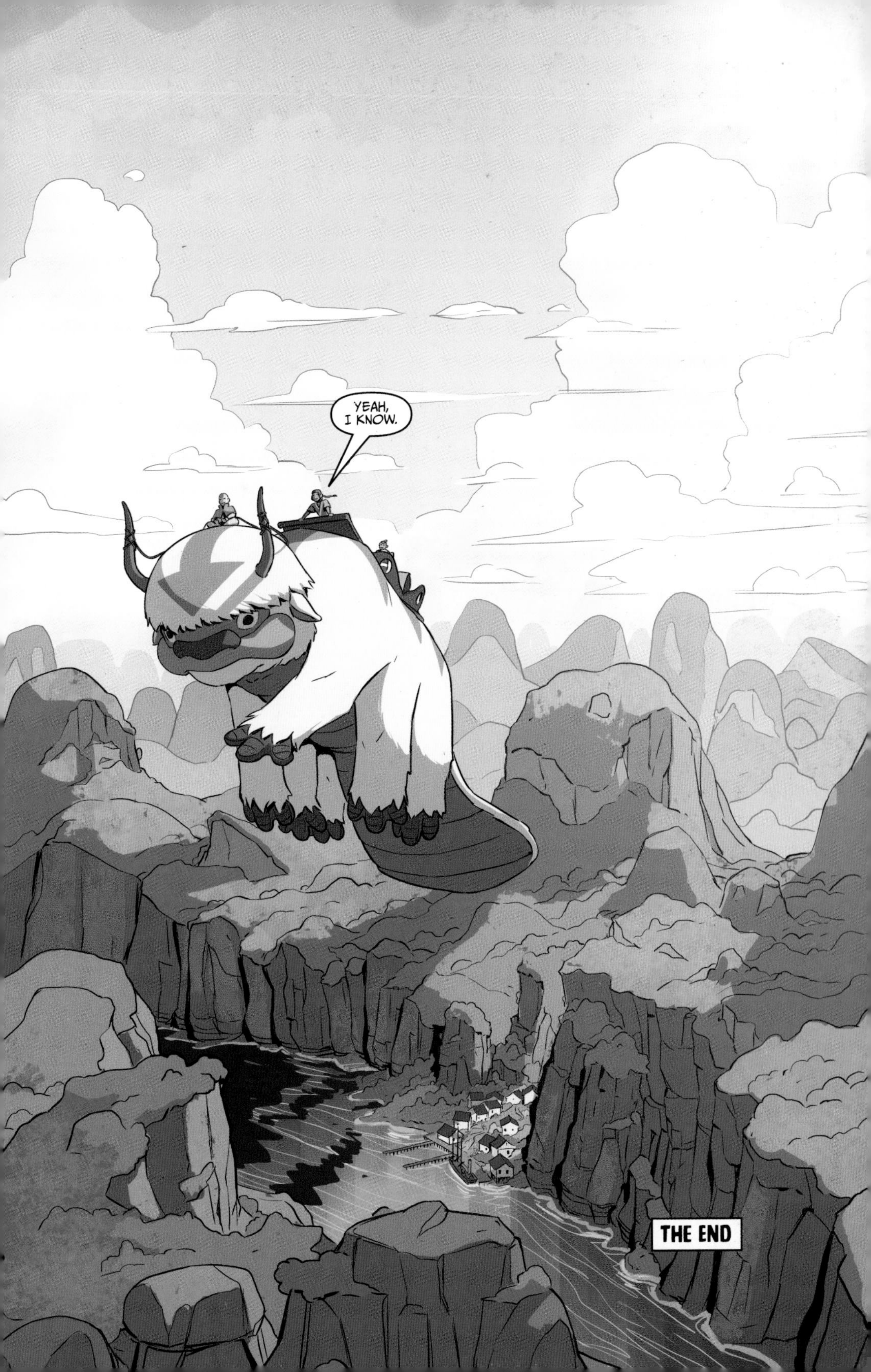
YEAH, I KNOW.
THE END

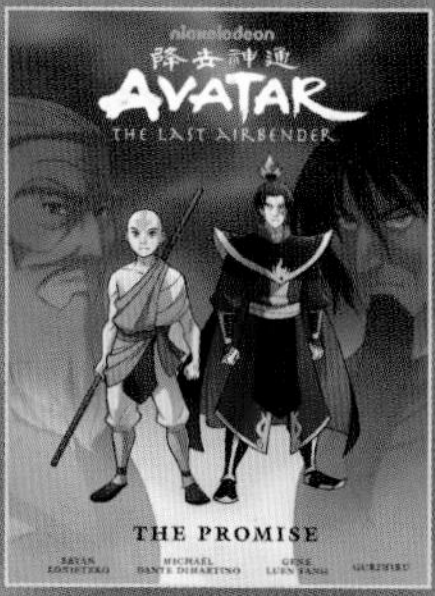
nickelodeon
AVATAR
THE LAST AIRBENDER
THE PROMISE

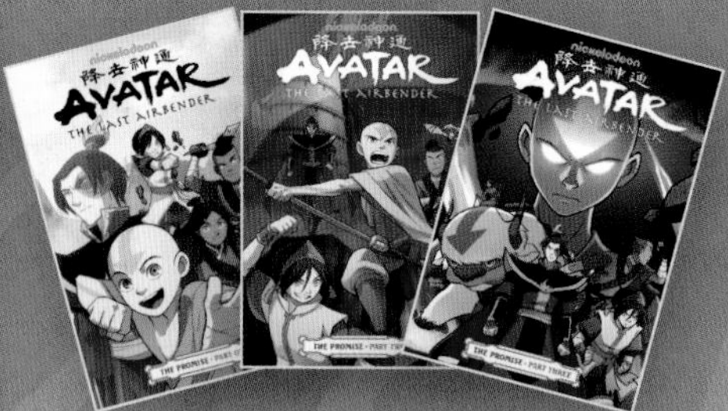
nickelodeon
AVATAR
THE LAST AIRBENDER

Avatar: The Last Airbender—The Promise Library Edition
978-1-61655-074-5 $39.99

Avatar: The Last Airbender—The Promise Part 1
978-1-59582-811-8 $10.99

Avatar: The Last Airbender—The Promise Part 2
978-1-59582-875-0 $10.99

Avatar: The Last Airbender—The Promise Part 3
978-1-59582-941-2 $10.99

Avatar: The Last Airbender—The Search Library Edition
978-1-61655-226-8 $39.99

Avatar: The Last Airbender—The Search Part 1
978-1-61655-054-7 $10.99

Avatar: The Last Airbender—The Search Part 2
978-1-61655-190-2 $10.99

Avatar: The Last Airbender—The Search Part 3
978-1-61655-184-1 $10.99

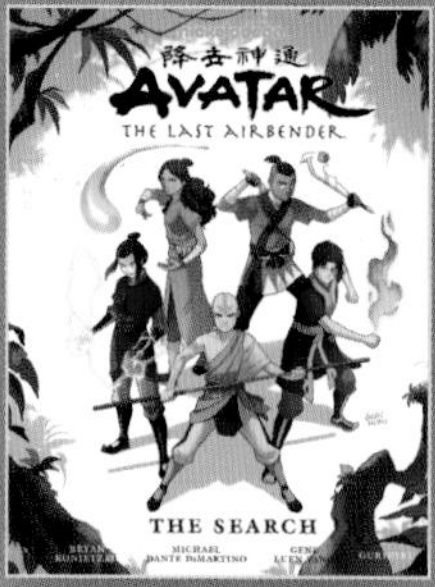
AVATAR
THE LAST AIRBENDER
THE SEARCH

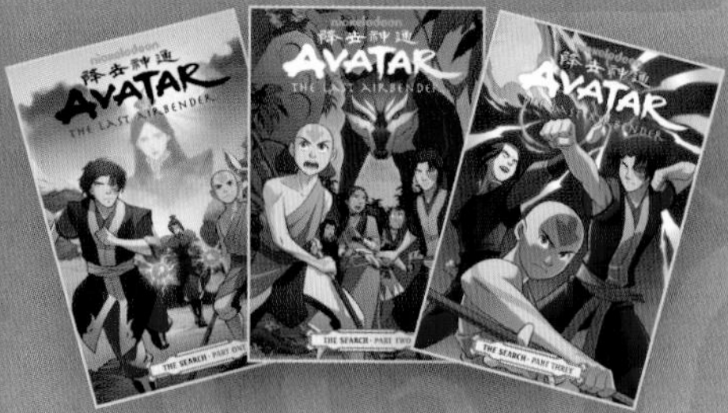
nickelodeon
AVATAR
THE LAST AIRBENDER

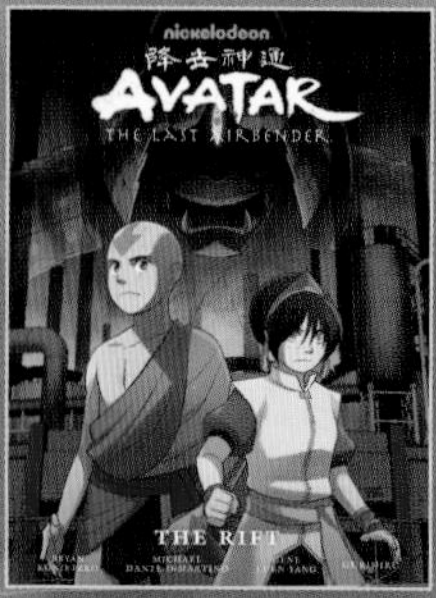
nickelodeon
AVATAR
THE LAST AIRBENDER
THE RIFT

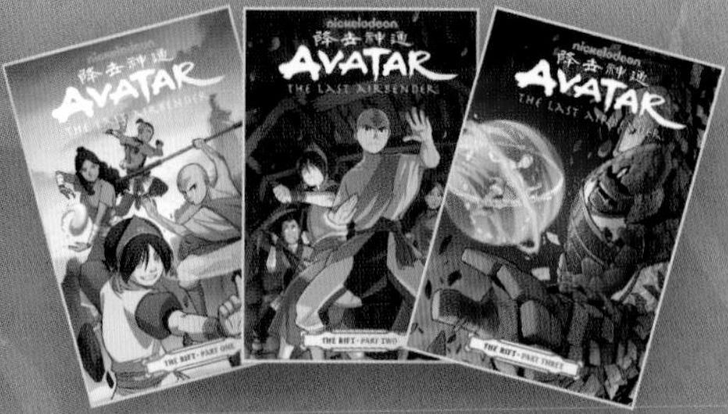
nickelodeon
AVATAR
THE LAST AIRBENDER

Avatar: The Last Airbender—The Rift Library Edition
978-1-61655-550-4 $39.99

Avatar: The Last Airbender—The Rift Part 1
978-1-61655-295-4 $10.99

Avatar: The Last Airbender—The Rift Part 2
978-1-61655-296-1 $10.99

Avatar: The Last Airbender—The Rift Part 3
978-1-61655-297-8 $10.99

Avatar: The Last Airbender—Smoke and Shadow Library Edition
978-1-50670-013-7 $39.99

Avatar: The Last Airbender—Smoke and Shadow Part 1
978-1-61655-761-4 $10.99

Avatar: The Last Airbender—Smoke and Shadow Part 2
978-1-61655-790-4 $10.99

Avatar: The Last Airbender—Smoke and Shadow Part 3
978-1-61655-838-3 $10.99

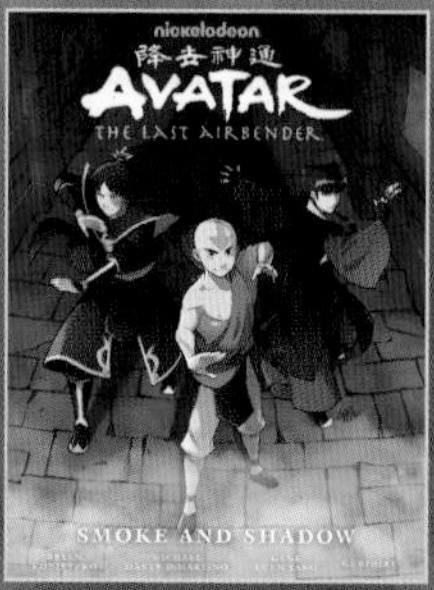
nickelodeon
AVATAR
THE LAST AIRBENDER
SMOKE AND SHADOW

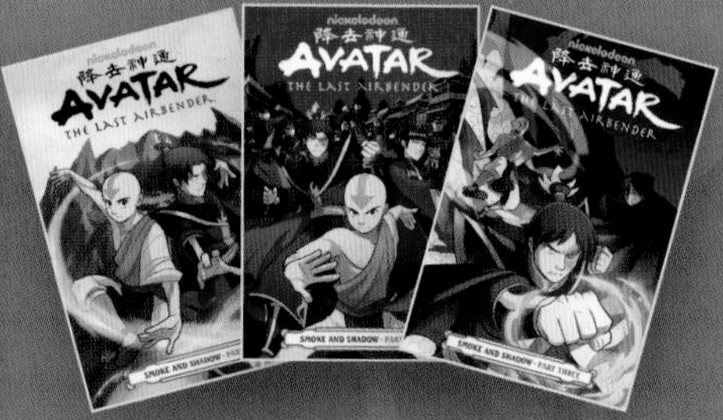
nickelodeon
AVATAR
THE LAST AIRBENDER